# Into My Heart

## The Mystical
## Journey
## of a
## Midwestern
## Christian
## Woman

Lucy Klemaier

INTO MY HEART

Published by
Human Sun Media

Book design by Deborah Perdue,
www.illuminationgraphics.com
Front cover image courtesy of www.shutterstock.com

Paperback ISBN: 978-0-692-86681-8
Ebook ISBN: 978-1-5323-3795-6

*I dedicate this book first and foremost to
Saniel and Linda Groves-Bonder who opened the door
into my heart's transformation.*

*To my husband, Carl, who never let me doubt myself.*

*To my daughter, Kate, and her husband, Keith
Nightlinger, and my grandchildren, Brady, and
Annelise for the inspiration to write "my story."*

# FOREWORD

*L*ucy Klemaier is a kind of spiritual Grandma Moses. Now a grandmother herself, she has for many decades undergone a spontaneous journey in Spirit that has exposed her to multiple traditions, teachings, teachers and influences outside the Protestant Christianity of her early life. Here, for all our benefit, she has turned the far-ranging events of her mystical adventure into this gem of a life-story to date. And here's why Grandma Moses comes to mind: Lucy tells her story with a natural innocence that, to me, is a kind of pure folk art.

I should tell you, I'm not a dispassionate, supposedly objective observer. Hardly. I helped encourage Lucy to write the book and suggested some of the fine professional book people who helped her craft the best version of her story she could and bring it into publication. The publishing imprint, Human Sun Media, is part of my wife Linda's and my Human Sun Institute.

More than that, I figure personally in the story. I first met Lucy and Carl as a spiritual teacher. Our interactions and the spiritual work I founded, known as Waking Down® or Waking Down in Mutuality®, are part of Lucy's odyssey.

Even more than that, I'm a passionate fan of this book and I hope it reaches and touches many, many people. Because what happened between Lucy's first, awkward efforts to write her story and what has emerged (without my active involvement until a late proofreading) is a marvel.

As I read, I was startled again and again by the simple purity of her voice, the unforced power of her imagery, her instinctual rhythms that keep grounding our encounter with her profound mystical transformations in the soil and the soul of everyday life in America's Heartland.

As moving and heart-full as her devotional openings and dark nights of the soul and her daring intuitions of divine spiritual identity are her renderings of the lives and trials of her rural Illinois forebears ... her descriptions of kernels of corn shining gold in the setting sun as her father ladled it out to the hogs on their farm ... her accounts of her struggles to find and speak her truth even when it turned friends and neighbors against her – and much more of the stuff of a life with lots of dirt under fingernails and lots of meals handcooked with all her heart and served, both when she was younger and even today, to lots and lots of grateful people.

Please read this book. Find out how Lucy has fared with the struggle between her outward-facing Martha and her deep inner Mary. (If you don't know what that reference points to, you will soon learn.)

I have to offer a prayer: I hope this book gets picked up by a publisher who can do justice to it. And, I pray that someone else someday writes a truly fitting foreword. Ideally, that person will not be part of Lucy's life already. She or he might be a trusted spiritual authority to many others. Someone whose words, then, far better than mine, can ensure potential readers that Lucy herself has become a trustable speaker to our hearts and souls with a poignant, unique, and empowering story to tell.

Saniel Bonder
Sonoma, California
February 8, 2017

# CHAPTER 1

## Chicken Pie Supper

*At* noon on the last Saturday in October 1998, I was standing over the old black Viking stove in the church kitchen stirring gravy. I had been there since eight that morning, working on the final preparations for our annual fundraiser chicken pie supper. The five others in the kitchen crew had arrived throughout the morning. We, White Hall Methodist women, had a reputation for serving the best chicken pie in the county. In a few hours about one hundred and fifty townsfolk would stream in expecting another delicious supper.

On Friday after teaching all day, I rushed to the church to help make mounds of slaw, peel piles of potatoes, and set up fifteen tables for those eating, plus one table for the drinks, one for the pies, and two for the buffet. It had taken a year's discussion to convince the older ladies to serve buffet style. The final agreement came after it was pointed out that smorgasbords were popular spots even with seniors. Most people were accustomed to carrying their own food. When we were finished, the fellowship hall looked inviting with the new burgundy tablecloths on each table, lavender mums in full bloom, and the children's construction paper leaves strung on colorful rag strips down the center of each table. When I got home at eight I still had to bake two Kentucky Derby pies, my specialty, and make two cranberry salads. I couldn't skip the pies. I could envision my older cousin at the dessert table with its luscious array of pumpkin, cherry, apple, and lemon pies, looking for my pecan and chocolate chip delight. I did allow myself the "shortcut" of store bought crusts and canned cranberries. It was nearly eleven when I fell into bed.

My friend Gail and I had just finished rolling out three hundred biscuits. At least we hadn't had to have the old argument about whether or not to cook old hens. Our generation made the decision to purchase frozen chopped chicken from the Schwan's man, ready to add to the other ingredients. We would not be slaughtering and plucking chickens like our grandmothers and mothers had done.

How many of these suppers had I helped with? I was coming up on my fiftieth birthday. From the time I was old enough to go door-to-door selling tickets at age nine, I had been involved. It had been fun then. I got a "free" supper if I sold ten tickets. Back then the kitchen had been swarming with helpers. The teenagers and young adults would help serve the plates as the women in the kitchen dished them up. The men washed, dried, and put away all the dishes. But I had had a glimpse of how stressful it could be for those in charge. One night I saw mother comforting the poor chairwoman who was sitting in the corner by the stove, broken down in tears from exhaustion and also relief that it was over. Maizie was a vivacious, energetic woman, never daunted, but the responsibility and the work of that long day and the days of preparation beforehand had finally gotten to her. She had reached her breaking point.

I never saw my mother cry over her church labors, but I watched her frustration mounting through the years. When I returned home after ten years away, my mother soon saw both of us caught up in the endless demands of church work. As matriarch of the group, she tried to tell the few ladies who were left to do the work, most of them in their fifties and sixties (my mother was seventy-five), that we should stop doing the supper. She told me directly, "I don't want you to have to work as hard as I've done all these years." No one else was willing to agree to give up hosting the supper, even with our dwindling number of cooks. How could we dare break with tradition and stop serving this dinner? Her plea was met with assurance that we could go on and would find more volunteers. My mother's advancing age limited her ability to help much after that, but I kept on as I had been, burying my frustration. Why did I continue to exhaust myself? When would I learn to say no? Why couldn't I say no?

In the early years of mother's involvement in the church, serving dinners had been a necessity in order to pay the pastor, keep the lights on, and heat the huge sanctuary. Now raising money was no longer such an urgent matter. The members' giving was sufficient to pay the bills. But something I have noticed about most pastors is that they want to keep the congregants working for each new project, under the assumption that we will have a greater appreciation for its worth because of our efforts.

Our minister had his eye on restoring the sanctuary to its former glory. Although we had at that point received a large unexpected inheritance, we would start from scratch on fundraising for this undertaking. It seemed that the building fund was always deficient.

About the time my friend Brenda and I were beginning to worry, as we did every year, about the non-thickening gravy, the minister popped in with my next task. Would I organize and serve the weekly community Advent breakfasts? That would mean I would have to be at the church to get the coffee started and set out all the food before 6:00 a.m. for the five weeks before Christmas. Anger welled up inside me. Had he been here all day helping to make this supper a success?

Since this minister's arrival five years before, in 1993, there had been an endless string of dinners, salad luncheons, and potlucks. New events had been added. Now we had a Maundy Thursday dinner, in addition to Good Friday and Easter Sunrise service and breakfast, plus the regular Easter service. As church organist, I was responsible for the music at these services. And as president of our local United Methodist Women, I was in charge of the meals. Then in 1998 our church celebrated 175 years of ministry. We had hosted a successful Heritage dinner in the spring and had another full day of festivities scheduled in two weeks. The month before the current chicken pie supper, I had opened my home for a house tour as part of our celebration. Naturally, that had entailed weeks of cleaning the house and yard. I had scurried around to select new bedspreads and hang new living room curtains. The bathroom had needed a fresh coat of paint. I had scrubbed the deck and refurbished the flower boxes at the back door. That night after the tour, I had collapsed on the couch. I had often heard mother say, "I'm so tired, I don't know my name!" I knew what she meant.

In that moment at the stove, I felt my heart start to pound, I could feel the heat rise to my flushed cheeks and something snapped. After years of hardly letting myself think such thoughts, much less voice them, I found myself saying, "The next minister isn't going to know I can do this."

He did a double take, a look of shock on his face at my uncharacteristic boldness. He said nothing, however. No "I'm sorry, I see you're busy right now" or "We'll talk later "or "I'll ask Jane to be in charge." Without a word, he walked out of the kitchen.

I, of course, immediately felt guilty. But Brenda, standing beside me at the stove adding more thickener to the gravy, had made an affirmative grunt at my outburst. She assured me I had nothing to feel guilty about.

I was too busy to fret about it for long, but all of a sudden I felt exhausted. I can work all day and not feel tired, but conflict is draining for me. Why hadn't I kept quiet like I always did? I avoided him the rest of the day. Or did he avoid me?

But by morning I had to get over my anger. It was Sunday and there was no way we could avoid each other. I found my special bulletin marked with my cues for the service as usual on the organ bench. When he came in from his first service we exchanged a brief hello. There was no time to discuss our differences then, not that we would have. That would have involved, perhaps, a conflict which I would have avoided at all costs, or an apology which neither one of us was prepared to offer. I knew I was going to do the breakfasts, even as I was having my outburst. As I sat in the choir loft that morning, I realized he often was as stressed out as I had been the night before, even if by his own design. In fact he had been near death with a mysterious heart infection eight months prior. He had returned in August after six months away. In his absence, we had carried out all he had set out for us to do to celebrate our 175 years. After service, I approached him in the back of the sanctuary after the congregants had departed. Sheepishly, I told him I would do the breakfasts. He accepted my acquiescence without question and we settled on the details of the event. I recognized my pattern, when asked or invited to do something, I would do it. Next time I would leave out the complaint.

For ten years I had been the church organist and every year looked forward to our beautiful Christmas Eve candlelight service. It was my favorite service of the year. I loved looking out over the congregation as they left the pews to stand in front of the ornate stained glass windows that lined the sanctuary. In the glow of the candles, we sang "Silent Night." I could feel the presence of spirit. Playing our beautiful old pipe organ was like meditation to me. Its magnificent sound would fill the sanctuary. My soul would sing. In preparation for this year's service, I had been practicing special music since Thanksgiving.

A week before Christmas, the minister called me. "Hello," he said, then blurted out, "I'm going to have Pauline play for Christmas Eve service." I detected a smugness in his voice. I didn't hear the excuse he gave. I was trying not to cry. I said, "Oh…okay." Then I hung up.

Evidently, he was still unhappy with me. I wandered around the house with an empty feeling. I wasn't even angry…until later. I was just terribly hurt. I thought of all I had done for him. Then I started to doubt my ability. Did I not play well enough? Pauline, the organist at his second church, was a very accomplished musician.

Later that afternoon, as I stood at the kitchen sink doing the lunch dishes, I saw the local florist pull into the driveway. He emerged from the van carrying a lovely Christmas arrangement of red and white carnations with glittered pine cones and holly. The card read, "Merry Christmas" and was signed by the pastor. I saw it as his peace offering. In the five years I had known him, he had been a caring pastor and friend. He was sensitive enough to know how his words had landed in me.

We never talked about the incident. "I'm sorry" was not spoken, but he had reconsidered and I did play for the service. I don't know what he expected my reaction to be. Maybe he would have handled anger better than hurt and then felt justified in teaching me a lesson. Was he really sorry or just worried I would not play at all? The ungracious thought did run through my head, "I'll show you, don't ask me to do anything again." But that's not me. I'm too practical. I wouldn't do that because there was too much to be done and too few people to do the work. I was too enmeshed in carrying on in my mother's footsteps. She had worked tirelessly, so I would too. Most obviously, how could I blame him, when I allowed him to think he could call on me for everything?

That was the first and last time that I told him how I really felt.

After that I went back to being a good church-woman. But I felt myself disconnected from what I wanted to feel in my heart and what was happening in reality. I was caught up in a tradition that wasn't feeding me. What I was feeling and what I wanted to feel were opposed. Feeling angry and tired was not going to turn into joy and bliss. What could I do to feel and know that "Christ was within"? Where was my devotion? A month before my outburst, the minister had given a sermon on the scripture in Luke about Martha and Mary. I was so tired of being the "overworked, complaining" sister, Martha. We had the authority of Jesus's word in the verse that Mary, sitting at His feet, had chosen what was better and it would not be taken from her. But what was "it"? Somewhere deep inside of me I wanted to become Mary, even though at the time I didn't know what that meant entirely or what it would look like, or how it would change my life. The sermon hadn't addressed those issues. Were there other women in the congregation with a secret longing to become Mary? As I looked over the congregation all I could see were "Marthas."

After church that day, as I was helping put away the communion glasses and trays, my friend said to me, "That scripture always confuses me, in fact, it makes me mad! I want Jesus to praise Martha for her dedicated service. What did Mary do to gain His favor?" I asked myself that same question. The answer must lie in her desire to know and love Him deeply and her devotion to that quest. It was her deeper knowledge that here before her was the Master who was showing her the path to living fully as a being created in the likeness of God. Of course, the world needs "Marthas," but I began to realize that my life was being overtaken with obligations. Was my outburst an unconscious recognition of a need to take the time to discern the difference between Martha and Mary and then the integration of the two? The understanding of this difference has become a recognition of what my soul needed to manifest love into my heart and into the world to serve others. I could only undertake the quest to understand the truth of this recognition when I could learn to be the authentic child of God I was born to be. There was more than gravy cookin' at that stove.

The journey to becoming this authentic woman was taken over a lifetime, a very ordinary lifetime. I characterized myself as a shy child, but I realize a better description would be reserved and quiet. My pattern from the beginning was "keep quiet until you know for sure." Throughout my life this pattern was true in all my interactions. I was a back-row kind of person. The voice in my head said, "Don't reveal your ignorance, don't answer until you're absolutely sure of the answer, don't ask any dumb questions, and don't try to perform until you know you can." I wanted to be the best because that meant approval. So I covered up my authentic self and took on "I'm shy, don't judge me. I'm going to sit here in my quiet shyness and figure this out on my own. I won't offer until I'm sure of the answer. Then you can't judge me." Martha was afraid of being judged as inadequate, while Mary knew in her being that devotion and love, not "doing" were of far greater importance. Judging by others did not touch her. She could act without guilt. Could I ever learn to do this?

While I was being the right-hand Martha to each new pastor, I also was carrying a belief in something else. Twenty-seven years earlier my husband, Carl, had introduced me to Eastern spirituality and mysticism. I knew there was more to spirituality than the religious structures taught in western Christianity, but I wasn't comfortable sharing the principles of Eastern mysticism. Any questioning or comparisons were met with blank stares at best and condemnation at worst from my fellow congregants. I wasn't confident of my knowledge or understanding of these principles at the time to talk freely. This esoteric knowledge of devotion to a guru, meditation, reincarnation, and many lifetimes of learning lessons to evolve one's spirit, would be foreign to most of those sitting around me in my church. My fellow

Methodists' knowledge of the transcendent was limited to its founder, John Wesley's experience of feeling his heart "strangely warmed." Yet I believed that I could have a direct experience of the Divine, I didn't know how to achieve it just yet. Looking back I can see the journey started with baby steps.

All along the way I had tiny glimpses of what this direct experience might mean. I think the world renowned sound healer, Tom Kenyon, expressed it best when he said, "The task of making contact with our infinite unbounded nature while operating within a reality of physical and cultural restraints is a Herculean effort." I see Mary as having made contact with that "infinite unbounded nature", Martha was struggling within the "reality of physical and cultural restraints", and the transformation process or integration of the two as "the Herculean effort." But before this "making contact with my infinite nature" was possible for me, I needed to examine my journey and understand how each step led me along the path. This discernment of the why, where, when, and how of life needed to make sense to me in order for me to find the effort and grace which has led me to the authenticity of my unbounded infinite nature.

I was set back on the spiritual path at birth, first through the stability of my ancestral karma, a concept that says we carry in our DNA the trauma or stability of our ancestors. I had no holocaust as with the Jews, or massacres as with the American Indian. Seven generations on both sides of my family lived in the rural community east of White Hall, Illinois, that came to be known as Lorton's Prairie. In the 1820's, after serving in the Revolutionary War, both of my Strang and Lorton great-great-great-grandfathers arrived in Greene County.

All ancestors since that time were rooted in the same section of Greene County, Illinois. Land grants signed by Presidents John Quincy Adams and Martin Van Buren hung proudly in our living room. These prairies were of rich fertile black loess soil carried down by the ancient glaciers that flattened and shaped Illinois. My dad was proud of the yields per acre of his soybeans, wheat, and corn, often the highest in the neighborhood. He raised stout, sleek, black Angus cattle and white belted Hampshire hogs.

I recognized, not only the stability of my ancestors in their everyday life, but also their spiritual stability as I read "Prairie Smoke," a journal based on the diaries of my great-great-great-grandmother, Jane Moses Wood Roodhouse, on my paternal side. Jane had left a comfortable life in Yorkshire, England because her second husband, Benjamin Roodhouse, and her three sons, had heard of "the vast lands and fortunes to be had in the New World." From her description of life in the early days of Greene County, I could feel the cold wind whipping across the prairie and know the need for hides up to the windows to tame the drafts. The long days of butchering hogs and making candles and soap were followed by long dark evenings, sewing by the fireside. Long evenings that were also "quite lonely in spirit." I could almost smell the smoke rising from the chimney that marked the cabin on the prairie for distant travelers. I could envision my ancestors riding across the field that was now my front yard. I looked out upon the same road that my great-great-grandfather, Abram Morrow, had traveled on horseback to court Mary Wood, Jane's daughter with Captain William Wood, her first husband and the love of her young life, who had been lost at sea. Her greatest legacy to me was her understanding of the eternal nature of our spiritual Beings. She reflected after the death of her husband, Benjamin, "I do not shed the bitter tears or do I grieve as I did for the Captain for I have grown wise in spiritual things. I do know these bodies are as dust but our spirit within these bodies are eternal and does go inviolate through the ages and knowing it to be thus I do not grieve. Too well do I know of those long months of grieving and how they did corrode mine heart."

Early Methodism shaped my ancestors' lives, lives of service and devotion, lives of ordinariness, common folk. In 1844, the famous Methodist circuit rider, Peter Cartwright, dedicated Jane's house, still standing today, south of White Hall. She says of that day, "The reverend Mister Cartwright with well-chosen words and an fine prayer did dedicate our home." After the guests had departed she gathered her household about her, "and I did pray to the Father to have peace and love abide within mine home and I did pray for His loving care and His protection for each one and at last I did offer up an great prayer of thanks for His tender care these many years of mine self an widow and mine children fatherless."

Another ancestor on my maternal side also helped establish Methodism in Greene County. My great grandfather, Allen Alexander Lorton, was known as a colorful character with a full head of pure white hair and Santa Claus beard, a Civil War veteran. In an historical sketch he had written for a reunion in 1935 held at Wesley Chapel on Lorton's Prairie, he described himself and our ancestors as home lovers who stayed close to the locality of their birth. They were aggressive pioneers, intrepid hunters, schooled in woodcraft, common people. The quote I loved best gave me insight about coming from a long line of Marthas, "They were mostly agriculturalists, tillers of the soil—obeying either willingly or unwillingly the scriptural injunction, "In the sweat of thy face, shalt thou eat bread."

Both the Lortons and Strangs appeared on the Wesley Chapel church rosters as teachers and elders since the time it was established in 1855. From christenings to funerals and marriages in between, this church had been their spiritual home. Both my parents had attended there. When dad was twelve years old, he had worked the team of horses used to break ground for an expansion of the building in 1922. Even my Irish Catholic maternal great grandmother, Mary Jane Cunningham Lee, sent her five children there because the nearest Catholic Church was too far away.

Eventually Wesley Chapel closed and my parents started attending church in town at the First Methodist Church in White Hall, my early spiritual home.

# CHAPTER 2

# Into My Heart

*B*ack then the church was also an important social connection. My parents' closest and most cherished lifelong friends were couples they met in the young adult Boosters Club. My mother, Lura Lee Lorton Strang, was the good Methodist woman, always available for the unending tasks of keeping the church going, working on fundraising dinners, being Sunday school superintendent, Woman's Society president, and board trustee and member. For her, it was a way of belonging and being accepted, and proving her worth, all proof of being bound to "Martha" ways.

She had started high school at the beginning of the Depression. Because it was too far for a young girl to travel alone and the road was often impassable, she stayed with a family in White Hall. In exchange for room and board, she babysat. There had been no question that she would attend high school, despite the difficulties. She had received many countywide awards for achievement in literature, history, writing, and spelling throughout grade school. Her education was important to her and to her parents. During the week she often attended activities at the Methodist church with classmates. On Fridays her father would make the trip to town in the wagon over the muddy, rutted road to take her home for the weekend. This story fascinated me because this was the same road we traveled every day for a ten minute trip to town.

While my mother graduated at the top of her class, my dad, William Howard Strang, was a less enthusiastic student. He preferred playing football and basketball. Though they had grown up in the same neighborhood, they had attended different country schools. Dad was three years older than mother, so they hadn't been in high school together. They started dating after a neighborhood get-together when they were in their early twenties. Oddly enough they had never spent much time together growing up. She often remarked, "If anyone had told me when I was growing up that I would marry Bill Strang, I would have told them they were crazy."

Most women in her generation got married and started a family after high school, if they attended high school at all, but mother felt she needed to be able to support herself. The world around her was sinking further into the Depression. Though college tuition was out of her reach, she was able to attend Brown's Business College in Jacksonville. She supported herself as a waitress at a hotel restaurant. Too timid to say anything, she watched the older waitresses take the tables with the businessmen staying at the hotel because they were usually big tippers. The school girls were left to wait on the locals who barely tipped at all. Then one day the manager announced that all tips would be pooled and shared. That helped her bank account, but not her relationship with the other ladies. I think how brave she was to take on a job she had no experience at and the frightening expenses of tuition in light of the condition of the country.

Dad had turned down a full football scholarship to Illinois College. His excuse had been that he had had enough of school, but the truth was, he was needed on the farm. He had been put to work at an early age, feeding the livestock and milking cows. Now at the beginning of the Depression his help was essential.

My parents continued to date on the weekends. He would borrow his neighbor's Model A Ford and take her back to school on Sunday evening. On one of these trips mother told him a young man had asked her to go to a movie. That was when he turned to her and said, "I really wish you wouldn't go with him." Until then she hadn't known how he felt about her for sure. That was his proposal. They were married in 1937 in the middle of the Depression.

They struggled along. Dad took care of the old grange block building, in exchange for their apartment rent, rising early on cold winter mornings to fire the boiler and making necessary repairs to the building, while at the same time he worked with his father on the farm. Mother was a secretary for the Home Advisor at the Greene County Farm Bureau office in Carrollton. After three years dad said to her, "We're going to move to the country and have a baby." She wasn't so sure. But that's what they did. They found a house and ground to rent down the road from his parents. My sister, Mary Lee, was born a week after Pearl Harbor was bombed. Since dad was a new father and also a farmer, he was not called into service during WWII.

I'm a baby boomer born in 1948 and my brother, Bill, followed two years later. The "fifties" was an easier time to grow up. Howdy Doody was the extent of our television watching. We could play safely and unsupervised around the farm. We would check in with mother off and on throughout the day. Foremost in my mind are memories of the long hot days of summer when my brother and I would wade in the creek and scoop up tadpoles in Mason jars, or slide down the muddy bank, our own private water park slide before we knew of such things. To keep cool we would play school or our favorite pretend activity, restaurant, in the basement. All my dolls and stuffed animals would double as customers. We would dig ashes out of the furnace and mix them with water to serve "sundaes" to our customers at the makeshift counter made of old boards and concrete blocks, a preview of my future days in my own restaurant.

My grandkids will not enjoy the independence of racing through the barn playing tag, climbing the ladder to the loft and swinging down on a rope. I watch my grandson "doing" these things while playing Minecraft on the iPad. Now he's trying to learn the fundamental skills of baseball surrounded by screaming, complaining adults. My brother and I played baseball for hours, just the two of us, in the shade of the ash trees in our side yard.

Of course, we fought like most siblings do. There was plenty of the "he's looking at me "or "he's touching my half of the seat," whining. Mother didn't mind our noise as long as it was a happy noise. But when she would cry out "God help me!" we knew we better straighten up fast. It was the closest she ever came to swearing.

Because of our age difference, my relationship with my sister was much different. She was out of the house at school or with her friends when I was little. Growing up she was our protector. In most pictures of the three of us, she has her arm around us, guiding us. I was too young to tag along in her world until I went to college. She was married and moved to Chicago while I was still in junior high school.

Around 1950 the busy and laborious life of taking over dad's family farm had occupied much of my parents' attention. Dad tore down the old two story farm house he was born in and built a snug cozy ranch type house for us. We would not be carrying heated bricks to bed to keep our feet warm like he had. His childhood bedroom had been upstairs on the northwest corner of that old drafty house, he often related the story of seeing his breath if he dared peek out of his warm feather bed during the cold winter.

He built most of the house himself with the help of his dear friend, Ward Ridings. He carefully selected each oak board for the hardwood floors and decided on two wide picture windows to open the house to the view of the fields.

During this time, mom and dad's church attendance had become sporadic because of the house construction and farming, but mostly due to the arrival of two babies in two years. Mother and Mary Lee often went without Bill and I. Keeping two toddlers corralled and quiet during services was not worth the effort. I'm sure Bill has forgotten the time after she did start taking us to church, when he was climbing around and fell over the back of the pew. It was one of the few times mother ever spanked him.

I can see myself sitting in the little Sunday school room between the kitchen and the fellowship hall where we gathered at the close of Sunday school. There were three rows of little chairs filled with children I didn't know. Bill sat in front of me in one of the smallest chairs. I picked a pink chair just my size. Mother had taken extra care to curl my hair and dress me in my special dress with tiny pink roses. I don't remember how many weeks we had been attending, but this first memory has become significant in my understanding of my journey.

Into my heart, in to my heart,
Come into my heart, Lord Jesus.
Come in today, come in to stay.
Come into my heart, Lord Jesus.

We sang this sweet song every Sunday as we bowed our heads, at the close of Sunday school. This was my first prayer even before I knew what prayer was. I would be starting first grade in a few months and thankfully my mother realized I needed exposure to other children. Sunday school would be a good place to start. I was a shy child. The only contact I had had with other kids was my little brother, Bill, and my older sister, Mary Lee. This was a whole new world for me, with other children to play with, tables and chairs just my size. I loved the children's Bible stories and coloring pages. But I had never sung with a group and did not know the songs. I remember being coaxed by the teacher to join in and I really wanted to. At first I sang under my breath. Then one Sunday a few weeks after first attending, I have the distinct memory of saying to myself, "Go ahead, you can sing this song. I'm going to sing this song today." So I did. The teacher must have praised me highly because the memory stuck.

I have been amazed to discover how integral this early memory has been to my life. I spent over fifty years within the walls of that church. It was my church home, one I was proud of, and would have been lost without, I now realize. I had never examined its significance as the beginning of my journey into my heart. The church had been a safe haven for me, but not because of its indoctrination of sin and salvation. Even as a small child I had rejected those concepts. When given the contradictory choice of a vengeful God and a loving Father, I chose the latter. Further, I chose to focus on Jesus. Early on I had a longing to know the Jesus in the songs, in the pictures, and the intricate stained glass windows. I rung as much spirituality out of it as I could. The fact that it had such a benign effect on me is significant in my ability to be open to all teachings that have played major roles in my life. The church was the first holding container of my spiritual Being while the task of living and learning the lessons my soul had set before me, and knowing my purpose was underway. Was Mary a key to remembering my purpose?

Mother kept us in Sunday school. We seldom missed. One Sunday morning we were in a minor car accident. As we approached the intersection of a crossroad about a mile from our house, we were broadsided and hit hard enough to spin us around into a ditch. My older sister grabbed Bill and me to keep us from flying out as the door fell open. We weren't hurt, just shaken a bit. We got out of the car and directly into our neighbor's car, as he had happened by, and went on to church. Later that afternoon my little brother started crying with a delayed emotional reaction. Mother said maybe it hadn't been such a good idea to go on to church. "Wasn't that silly to think we should go on to church as if nothing had happened," she commented later. But it was just what we did without question, carry on with no fanfare or drama.

The summer before my eighth birthday had been long and boring and out of the ordinary because both mother and dad had been sick with a virus. Mother spent most of July in bed. Then dad came down with the same illness in August. Something felt off. It seemed hard to play knowing they weren't up and about doing their normal activities. Because dad wasn't improving as mother finally did, he went to the doctor and got a chest X-ray.

"I know something is wrong. Why did dad look so concerned, as he went into that big dark, ugly building? I think they called it a sanitarium." As we sat in the hot car, my brother and I tried to behave. Mother was so quiet. I was old enough to know that whatever was going on would have a major impact on our family. We could immediately see the smile on dad's face as he came through the door and crossed the parking lot. "No TB or cancer!" he reported. In celebration we stopped to eat before going home. A Ranch House Restaurant hamburger, a rare treat, had never tasted so good. After that dad started attending church regularly. It was never shared if he thought his prayers had been answered or if he had made a promise to God to attend church, but he rarely missed after that. We all usually sat together in the eighth pew on the south side of the aisle. My Grandpa Strang always sat in the third pew on the north side. As steeped as we were in all this church tradition and attendance, neither dad or mother ever shared their beliefs or preached. My father was also a dedicated Mason who knew all the rituals by heart. I believe the mystical teachings and rituals had their effect on him, but he never shared his thoughts about them. I wonder now how he reconciled the mysticism with church beliefs.

One of the few times I remember mother saying anything about beliefs was after she had attended her brother's fundamentalist Southern Baptist church with his grandson and granddaughter. The preteen children had just lost their mother to suicide and were certainly in need of comforting, but the preacher delivered a scathing message about sin and hell and Satan, all the while peering down at these two children as they sat in the front pew. Mother was horrified and found the sermon offensive and its delivery aimed at Amy and Tom disgusting and mean. She asked her brother to speak up and do something about the dreadful message, or at least not subject them to it again. Neither of which pieces of advice were taken.

I realize now this lack of preaching left me free to find and follow my own path. I am thankful when I see people struggling with beliefs they were indoctrinated with in childhood. To them, any questioning is blamed on "Satan." They have beliefs of Heaven being a place up there, God being in heaven, concepts of a child's mind, yet perpetuated still. When Jesus said we could do all he could do and more, I wonder what people envisioned for themselves. It wasn't until I studied Unity teachings and its positive Christianity that I began to grasp this concept myself. Yet I never had a childlike faith of feeling powerless or a sinner or needing Jesus to die for my sins.

Church and family influence us surely, but then comes school.

# CHAPTER 3

## Freckle Faced and Shy

*It* is strangely familiar to touch back sixty years to that little freckled face girl in the grass green dress with white Peter Pan collar, getting on the school bus for the first time, feeling anxious yet excited. Beyond my Sunday school experience I had never been around any other children except my brother. I knew very little about letters and numbers and even less about the world. There was no public school kindergarten and only a few of my classmates had attended the private kindergarten at the Baptist church.

I immediately fell in love with my first grade teacher Mrs. Smith. Every other year I had a kind, warm grandmotherly type teacher, in between, not so much. I remember more of what I learned from my stricter teachers, but, perhaps because those are the only memories they left me with.

In first grade I was much too shy to even speak up when my lunch was lost, but Mrs. Smith noticed and gave me part of hers. She patiently taught me how to write my name which I proudly wrote on my bedstead, much to my mother's dismay. I remember the first word I learned to read was "look." I was thrilled to show mom and dad I knew the word on Look magazine. At first I confused six and seven. My new best friend, Beverly, knew all the numbers and I was determined to learn them quickly so that I wouldn't be sitting in that little semicircle of chairs waiting for extra instruction.

How naïve and backward I was. Today what I learned in first grade is now picked up easily for most children in preschool. It feels now like I was born an old unencumbered soul. I suffered no trauma, no indoctrination, just living a carefree simple upbringing, all circumstances that I view now as beneficial to evolving into the ordinary, Divine human that I was to become, indeed we are all meant to become. There were few issues to scratch away, no deep or lasting wounding experiences. Most of my fears were "normal" ones taken on by most children who have to get on in the world.

Yet fears that left me unable to fully become the authentic person I was meant to be until I faced the disappointments, fears, hurts, shame, and anxieties taken on just by growing up with parents, teachers, and friends with their own issues.

I wonder if DeWayne remembers the paddling he got in second grade. I do. The dreaded paddle that hung on a nail at the end of the blackboard, was a constant reminder to behave. But I hadn't noticed DeWayne misbehaving. I just knew Mrs. Sheppard was coming right toward me down my aisle. What had I done? Then she jerked DeWayne out of the seat directly behind me. The other kids snickered, but I wanted to cry from relief, or perhaps sympathy. This woman was unpredictable, and never pleased. In fact, she is the only teacher I had whose face I cannot recall.

The other second grade teacher, an old white haired spinster, Miss Jensen, would probably have been worse. She brings to mind the witch in "Hansel and Gretel." I can still feel her bony finger as she pushed me back in line with the other children. It was clear she didn't care that I was trying to tell her my mother did not want me to go outside for recess because I had been sick. If she didn't care what my mother said she certainly didn't want to hear from me.

My third grade teacher, Mrs. Bailey, was the ultimate grandmotherly type. Short and plump with salt and pepper hair and glasses. She loved to tell stories about her grandkids, Tonya, Tracia, Treea, and Timothy. They lived with her. Her daughter, the mother of the four "Ts", was a hard-looking young woman with bleached blonde hair and tattoos. I was fascinated by her appearance. It was hardly typical of the 1950's moms I knew. Their father was a truck driver, whose semi would occasionally be parked at Mrs. Bailey's house. I felt sorry for the kids not seeing their dad every day.

My mother said Mrs. Bailey was a guest at our dinner table every night. I retold every new story she shared each day. As she dished out the ice cream for dessert, I heard mother whisper to dad, "I wonder when she has time to teach?"

"Mrs. Bailey's favorite ice cream is butter pecan," I piped up.

I will always love Mrs. B, she saved me from the "meanest" teacher in the school, according to the kids. Mrs. Hughes, her black hair pulled back into a severe bun, rarely smiled. Sometimes at recess I played with Linda, a neighbor who rode the school bus with me, and her friend Karen, a town girl. They were a year older than me and were in "old lady Hughes's" class. That's what they called her.

One day, Linda, Karen, and I were swinging at noon recess when Donna, also a fellow bus rider, ran up and asked to join us. I was ready to say yes, but then Linda said no. Karen chimed in, too. Donna flipped her pretty, long chestnut pony tail and ran off, yelling, "I'm telling the teacher on you!" That's when we had the brilliant idea to write a hateful note to her. "We don't like you. We don't want to play with you. We hate you." Advice to all, never put it in writing! Before social media, this is what kids stupidly did. Today we would have texted her which is even more incriminating.

Later I learned that Linda and Karen had added a PS, "We hope you go to hell!" Somehow Mrs. Hughes took possession of the note. Her strict Baptist beliefs caused her to be outraged at the word hell. What little sinners we were! The next day I was taken into the hall with Mrs. Bailey and Donna's teacher, Mrs. Phillips. I was mortified and shaking, fighting back tears. I never told my parents about the incident. I remember my mother thinking I was sick that night. When Mrs. Phillips asked Donna to join us in the hall, we immediately made up. I overheard the two teachers wondering how they were going to handle the situation with Mrs. Hughes. She wanted her "pound of flesh" from me, too. I heard them say, "This is just what little girls do, one minute fighting, and the next back to being best friends." Then Mrs. Bailey said, "Run off now. Go play, it's OK." I can still feel the relief in my body at her words.

With Mrs. Bailey's help, we were able to convince Mrs. Hughes that I had had no part in the hell statement. So she granted me forgiveness. I think she felt I had been led astray and had learned my lesson. But poor Linda and Karen were sent to the principal's office and didn't see the playground for two weeks.

In fairness to Mrs. Hughes, when she became my fourth grade teacher, I discovered that if you followed her rules she was quite nice to you. There was certainly no time in her day for long-winded stories. I was able to redeem myself in her eyes. I showed her I was "a good little girl." But the incident sent fearful little me into hiding. I didn't resolve its effect on me until fifteen years later when I recalled the event with Mrs. Phillips who had become my teaching colleague. "Oh she should have left it alone, no big deal." She revealed to me she had found Mrs. Hughes hard to work with as well.

"Yippee! Extra recess!" That's what I remember about fifth grade. Mellow, mild mannered, Mrs. Bates sent those who were finished with their work to the playground while she tried her best to teach the other two-thirds of the class what we already knew. She never raised her voice or showed any frustration. She was calm in all circumstances, even the way she climbed the stairs was serene. The pressure of the previous year was relieved, I relished being the teacher's pet. There was nothing to prove, but not many challenges either.

The year before entering junior high I was in the academically high tracked classroom of Mrs. James. I can still hear her byline, "You'll thank me when you're in college!" She would roll the word college out of the back of her throat, then off her tongue. Then she would purse her wrinkled lips and smirk, all the while peering through her glasses, over her pointy witch nose. What did we sixth graders know of college? If we thought this was hard how would we survive college? In relating this story to my husband recently, we laughed until I had tears rolling. Then it hit me, was this the source of my thinking I couldn't finish college? Why did I think that? I was a National Honor Society student and sixth in my high school graduating class. In fact I would have graduated from college with a four point average, if not for the occasional mediocre grade in PE and a couple of math classes, plus the only D I ever received. That was thanks to the handsome and arrogant world history professor, Herbert Lasky, who strutted back and forth in front of the class in his expensive three piece suit, flipping ashes from his cigarette into the waste can. He didn't feel I had a grasp of Prussian history and he was probably right.

Was it Miss Jensen's bony finger I felt on my chest or the cold black eyes of Mrs. Hughes piercing my heart that set in motion the shame and anxiety and fear that forced me into the back row and the feelings of insecurity? Was that why I could not find my voice to speak with confidence? Yet I view my incidents of shame and anxiety as minor compared to the stories of others. Perhaps this illustrates that the primal feelings of shame and anxiety are there in each of us waiting to be triggered by small or large experiences. We are tied to the rules to avoid the shame and anxiety. Martha was living the only role she saw open to her as a woman which was to serve and follow those rules. Yet Mary dared to follow Jesus who was creating new rules, inclusive rules, revealing God's compassion rather than God's punishment. How had rules silenced me, if only in small ways?

# CHAPTER 4

## "You could do more"

*S*ince that first Sunday of finding my voice to sing "Into My Heart" I had found the key to feeding my soul. I knew every Sunday school song by heart and gathering at the end of Sunday school to sing them was my favorite time. I wanted to learn to play the piano that sat in our living room, rather than have mother yelling at Bill and me to stop pounding on the keys.

Finally, I was sitting at the grand piano in Mrs. Barnett's front parlor. She had told mother the year before that I could start lessons when I was in third grade. Mrs. Barnett was not like any other woman I'd known. She was tall and slender, elegant and dignified, her salt and pepper hair wound into a loose bun at the nape of her neck.

Above all, she was always patient. In the eight years of weekly lessons she never once lost her patience with me. Most of the time was spent on the lesson, but occasionally she would talk about her husband, Fleet, in passing. What a fascinating name! Sometimes I would hear him rustling the newspaper from the den. I don't recall him ever speaking to me, although he would smile at me. As I struggled to play the challenging pieces, I fell in love with classical music. Mrs. Barnett's praise was all I needed to keep going and try harder. She had long ago passed away when I started playing the church organ, but I often thought of her in gratitude and felt her presence. Would I have appreciated the significance of its glorious sound without her influence in my life?

I started beginner band when I was in fifth grade. All my friends were going to be in band, so that's what I wanted to do, too. My parents said, "Good, you can play your sister's saxophone."

She had bought the instrument with money she earned from the sale of her 4-H calf. Now that she had graduated from high school the sax was gathering dust in the closet. Of course, being kid-like, I didn't want to play the saxophone, I would have preferred the French horn. I played that saxophone. I don't know that had I put up a strong objection they would have let me choose my own instrument, but that was not an option. Getting a new instrument would not have been practical when we already had a perfectly fine one. I discovered that a lot of kids thought the saxophone was cool, so I became okay with it.

Our instructor, Mr. Jennings, was a mild mannered and kind young man. He had to be to listen to the squawking cacophony that usually characterizes a junior high band. I was content to sit in the third chair and play along. I owe my music appreciation and ability to distinguish the sounds of different instruments in a piece of music to these times.

Then on to high school and a new band teacher, Mr. Mucci. He was a fiery Italian, with great energy and emotion. He turned us into a band to be proud of. Our trumpet section had depth all the way to the sixth or seventh chair. Once again I was happy in the fourth chair of the sax section. I wasn't going to be challenging any one to move up. I didn't want to be playing any solos, even for a few bars. We became one of the best marching and concert bands in the area. Mr. Mucci had confidence in our ability to take on the most difficult music. It was rare that we ever got less than a first at music contest.

One day I was standing at his desk with my friend, Sherry, who was going to contest with a trumpet solo. He wanted to know why I wasn't doing the same. In my mind I was thinking I was not good enough to do that. That was when he said the words that have rung in my head ever since. "You could do more." Four words that I have never forgotten. At the time I thought, "Wow is he right?" I thought I was doing all I could. I just shrugged and he rolled his eyes and sighed. He was accustomed to unresponsive teenagers.

But I suppose I did hear his words as an invitation when I joined stage band. We played at every basketball game. We were the backbone for every musical. I can't imagine my life without the in-depth knowledge of music I learned from him. I feel regret that I didn't tell him how much those words spurred me on. Not so much at the time, but now I recognize them as monumental advice for living an authentic life. I can see now every experience where I challenged myself to do more. Doing more, seeing where I can do more, I realize that more translates into the truth of who I am on a deeper level.

The auditorium was filled with hundreds of junior high and high school students. The sound of our voices blended into a magnificent performance. We had gathered together at an all–state music conference at the University of Illinois. Nervously I took my seat in the alto section. I was relieved to realize that my years of piano helped me sing the alto part. Each day I sang a little louder and stronger when I found that the girl next to me was following my lead.

My dear friend and later teaching colleague, Mrs. Martin, was also my vocal music teacher from sixth grade until I graduated from high school. She let me know I could do more without saying a word. I was surprised and thrilled that she selected me to go to that all-state conference when I was in sixth grade. I see now it was not my singing ability she wanted to boost, but my confidence. From then on I was never afraid to try out for any singing group. Although I never ever sang a solo. Being of a modest, shy nature, I was satisfied with being part of the group.

My happiest high school memories center on band and vocal music. I was not athletic. Maybe I would have been if basketball, soccer, or softball had been offered, but they were not an option for girls at that time in our rural area. Only five girls were chosen to be cheerleaders for each boys' team. That was the extent of the athletics for girls. So music was our place to shine. Today's kids don't have the luxury of spending two class periods per day on music. I know my life has been enriched by music, not algebra II.

# CHAPTER 5

## "Do you have a name?"

*A*s I walked along Seventh Street on the east side of campus, I felt an excitement inside tempered with a fear of the unknown. I knew these next four years would shape my life. Would I be successful in earning a degree? Was my future husband here already? At that time I had no conscious knowledge of karma or spiritual paths. I started college at Eastern Illinois University at Charleston, Illinois in the fall of 1966 as an elementary education major. I chose El Ed by process of elimination. I didn't want to be a nurse. My experience as a candy striper in our small hospital in White Hall had been valuable in showing me I wasn't comfortable taking care of sick people. Secretary or social worker did not appeal to me either. Teaching seemed the most doable and a good profession for a woman. There was very little career counseling in my high school. These professions were the only ones I was familiar with. I had no knowledge of the business world nor any interest. Journalism or advertising would not have appealed to me. Those were city professions. The women's liberation movement, just getting started, might have provided more possibilities or spurred other interests for me, but I had grown up when girls weren't even offered sports.

The sixties…the Vietnam War, counterculture, love-ins, long hair, mini-skirts, psychedelic music, Led Zeppelin, Bob Dylan, and The Beatles, and mysticism …an exciting and pivotal time in America. Eastern Illinois University was a relatively conservative school. The student body was made up of mostly small town farm kids. It had been my thought that it was hard to be a hippie at Eastern. I really didn't know any "hippie types" until that March day in 1969 in Coleman Hall when I met Carl, spring quarter of my junior year. I see now that it was the fulfillment of a sacred contract that we would come into this lifetime together. That feeling of "I know you" in the intimacy and trust we shared from the first day was not based on a chance acquaintance. Our paths to the same spiritual goal have weaved in and out of our lives for over fifty years.

I had never dropped and added a course since I had started college, but three days into the quarter I added a Russian literature class. I entered the classroom and sat in the next to the last row next to the window. That's when Carl leaned forward from the back row and whispered, "Do you have a name?" I just smiled and pointed to my name on my notebook. He said it was my quiet assured presence and my beautiful long auburn hair that attracted him.

I thought he was kind of cute with his dark hair and mustache. His pick-up line had amused me. We went to the student union together after class along with two of his friends who were in the class, too. We met another of his friends there. It was appealing to be part of a new group. Up until then I had hung around with my old friends from home or my roommate. I had dated a handful of guys none of whom seemed to care about me enough.

Carl didn't look like a long haired hippie, but more of a worker of the world type leftist in a blue work shirt and jeans, fitting with his family background of coal miners and early labor union supporters. Quite the contrast to my upbringing in a conservative rural farm community. I wasn't that interested in politics and my attraction to him was not a rebellion of any kind or a reaction to my world. I soon learned he was active in the counterculture of anti-war and political protest. He had met Abbie Hoffman at a Doors concert after attending an anti-war teach-in at the University of Chicago. On campus he had taken part in several anti-war demonstrations. I didn't join any of these activities, but I wasn't put off by his participation either.

I was more attracted to his intelligence, the way he could put ideas together and his ability to speak his mind. He was a philosophy major. I hadn't known that many deep thinkers, if any. He was different from anyone I knew. He loved being surrounded by books. I often met him at the Lincoln Bookstore across from Old Main where he worked, shelving books and waiting on customers. He would share what he was reading with me. The beginning of our extensive library, filled with esoteric, mystical, and scientific books centered on enlightenment and self-realization, started here. This was where the roots of his, and then my, spiritual seeking began.

His philosophy professor, Stuart Penn, became a dear friend as well, and introduced Carl to Eastern spirituality. One of his English professors, George Colby, was a great influence on our later decision to be initiated into Radha Swami, yoga of the sound current. The door to the world of mysticism had been opened.

At this time, Timothy Leary was conducting his LSD experiments at Harvard along with Richard Alpert, later called Ram Dass. Alpert's book *Be Here Now,* written a year or so later, became the "counterculture bible." These were the men who were paving the way for Eastern spiritual thought to enter the minds of westerners.

Carl's experience with LSD had shown him there is indeed another reality and much more to our Being and consciousness. I was too afraid to try LSD. I just took his word for it.

Besides remembering my struggle to read and make sense of Tolstoy's *War and Peace,* my memories of our early times together were clouded by our fear of him having to go to the Vietnam War. It was raging throughout that time. The evening news was one horrific report after another of battles and war dead counts. It was looming on the horizon for us.

But that spring we partied. Carl was living at a house on the lake a few miles from campus. I found it a welcomed refuge from dorm life. That was where I met his parents. My future mother-in-law was a plump little Italian, high strung and full of chatter. When she would arrive on a Sunday, the car would be packed with her famous homemade lasagna, delicious thick breaded pork chops, cinnamon bread and cookies from her favorite

Italian bakery, and my favorite, fried artichokes. Carl's father, from a long line of stoic German stock, was quiet and quite similar in demeanor to my own father. His parents both seemed to approve of me at the time and later confessed they had been surprised, but happy, Carl had taken up with such a "normal girl." They never stayed long on these Sunday visits, Claudia didn't like leaving home and was anxious to get back there as soon as possible.

This was Carl's last quarter before graduation. With his help I was able to write satisfactory papers on *War and Peace* and *The Brothers Karamazov,* for a decent enough grade. To me there was nothing drier than this literature, but the political themes intrigued Carl. He, of course, got an "A." He was totally frustrated in his Logic course, however. We were even afraid it might jeopardize his graduating, but he managed to squeeze out a passing grade. We celebrated the end of the quarter with a big bonfire on the lakeshore, taking delight in watching *War and Peace* and his Logic textbook go up in flames!

I was sad for us to part for the summer, but Carl had decided to study for a master's degree  and would start the summer quarter and return in the fall. I had taken a job as a nanny in the Chicago suburb of Northbrook for the summer. We exchanged letters and I went to Charleston to visit once over the summer. In the fall we were reunited. I moved out of the dorm to get away from a new freshman roommate who rose at the crack of dawn to make sure she got her makeup just right. I, on the other hand, slept in, needing only twenty minutes to get to class at ten. I shared an apartment with Karen, a girlfriend of one of Carl's roommates. He rented a room with his married friends, Robert and Dianne, down the street from me, along with his buddies, Harry and Greg.

The crisp fall days flew by quickly. The ginkgoes in the quadrangle on campus dropped their leaves in one day as they did each year. I finished up my course work and prepared to do student teaching at Sullivan, Illinois in the spring. Looked like I would graduate after all!

Our somewhat carefree days were about to end. December 1969, the draft, it was the first since World War II. Anxiously Carl, Harry, and Greg waited as the announcement of the lottery results came over the radio. Robert's new baby, Amy, would make him exempt. Carl's birthday came up number 27. His friends' numbers were much farther down the list. We were devastated. I sat on his lap and cried. He applied for conscientious objector status, but was denied. The thought of going to Canada was too daunting.

The first notice for a physical came in January. One cold morning in February he was up early to catch the bus in Effingham to go to St. Louis for his first military physical. Armed with whiskey, LSD, and fear, he went, but was not accepted, yet he also was not rejected. Later that summer he went a second time, same result. Desperately, he made the decision to join the Peace Corps and would be trained to become a English as a Second Language teacher in Korea.

Soon after my graduation in May 1970, I very appreciatively accepted an offer to teach first grade at my former elementary school in White Hall. Many of my old teachers were still teaching. I was privileged to teach with my beloved first grade teacher, Mrs. Smith. Her mentoring was equal to all the education courses I had taken in college. Though I may have backed into becoming a teacher in a lukewarm fashion, I discovered I loved it. I was fascinated watching each child learn to read in his own way. We implemented Alpha One, a comprehensive phonics program taught through stories of its whimsical letter people that year. My students could go to the board and write most any word I called out. I was thankful to be busy when Carl left for his training and two years of Peace Corps service.

During Christmas vacation, my trip to Hilo, Hawaii, where he was training, was a bittersweet interlude for us.

I remember the stewardess on my flight expressing surprise that I did not deplane in Honolulu. That was where soldiers from Vietnam went for R&R. Many young women met their husbands, fiancés, and boyfriends there. When we parted I had the comfort of knowing he wasn't going into a war zone. He would not come home maimed, or worse, not at all.

When the phone rang that cold February day in 1971, I was surprised to hear Carl's voice. "I'm coming home and I want to get married." Even though we knew coming home meant facing the draft board once again, staying in Korea had proved to be too difficult. The austere accommodations with a hole in the floor for a toilet and Kimchi for every meal was too much for a Midwestern boy. Learning Korean proved almost impossible, as well.

Shortly after his return there was one last ordeal to endure at the army induction center in St. Louis. This time he was prepared to refuse induction. Oddly enough the only advice his World War II veteran father ever gave him in his entire life was to try to get out of being inducted. Armed once again with whiskey and LSD, he "convinced" the army psychiatrist he was not a good candidate. Perhaps when Carl disparaged Nixon in front of a line of recruits and was threatened with five year's imprisonment, the doctor decided he was too much trouble and would indeed be a poor soldier. War, guns, and killing were not in his karma this lifetime. While in Hawaii training for the Peace Corps, Carl saved a young man from drowning. Looking back he felt perhaps that was the reason he was there instead of boot camp at Fort Leonard Wood.

Preparations for our Labor Day wedding began. Mother and I had such fun selecting my gorgeous ecru bridal gown with a Victorian collar and lace front panel. There was no question that we would be married in my church, but first we had to satisfy Carl's mother with a visit to her priest. Carl did not care if mother and I met with the priest or not, but this dispensation was important to his mother. The priest asked about my faith and I answered as best I could. I had always just taken my beliefs for granted and never really formulated any explanation before. Then came the question that totally shocked me. "Weren't you taught in Sunday school that your religion is better than any other? Don't you think that Catholics and people in other denominations are going to hell?"

"Certainly not!" I replied. "My church is tolerant of all religions. I was never taught that it was better."

"Really?" he questioned. I could tell he didn't believe

me. I concluded he didn't know much about Methodism. I tried to explain to him that my Methodism was quite middle of the road and our sermons and lessons were mostly about God's love as found in the New Testament. He would have been surprised to know how little I had even heard the word hell growing up. I don't remember mother saying anything, but we had a good laugh about it after the priest sent us on our way with "permission" for Carl to be married in my church.

September 4, 1971 was a sunny warm day. At 11:00 a.m. we were married by Rev. William Werner. As a new pastor, it was his first time performing a wedding ceremony. He was more nervous than we were. I remember him looking at us very intently and deliberately as we repeated our vows. None of us wanted any mistakes. The reception at home on the farm was lovely. Mother and dad had enlisted the help of some of their closest friends to prepare the buffet. I especially remember the cream cheese frosted sandwich loaf and dainty pastel petit fours. We cut the three tiered cake topped with fresh yellow roses in front of the picture window in the living room. One of my favorite pictures of the day was the view behind us of the ripening cornfield.

Then on to the evening reception in Springfield with all of Carl's parents' friends and relatives. The traditional

Italian party with lasagna and meatballs and a second wedding cake was quite the contrast to the quiet, reserved buffet at my house earlier in the day. We all threw ourselves into the occasion, though. One of my most cherished pictures is of mother and dad dancing, something I had never seen them do. Carl's parents, famous for their polka, often went dancing, but not mine.

No time for a honeymoon. I was back teaching my first graders Tuesday morning. Carl was off commuting to Southern Illinois University in Edwardsville to complete courses for a teaching certificate. We rented an upstairs apartment in the home of Meda Hayes on Carrollton Street in White Hall for $60 a month. Our long quiet winter nights were spent reading or playing Yahtzee or listening to music. We had no television. Carl also wrote his English Master's thesis on existentialism in Ernest Hemingway's works that year. I would go home for lunch on most days. Carl would have a vegetarian delight prepared. His favorite was miso soup with a meager portion of carrots floating around in the brown broth. I was sooo hungry.

Then in January 1972 came our initiation into Radha Swami, yoga of the sound current with living Master, Charan Singh. Carl had been introduced to Radha Swami by his English professor, George Colby. They became friends and obviously had a karmic connection which in turn also included me. Shortly after we were married, we had written personal letters to Charan Singh who lived in Beas, India, to receive permission for initiation. There were only two times a year that initiations were performed at the satsang, or meeting, in Chicago, the closest location to us. We made the four hour trip from White Hall to the YMCA building at the corner of Superior and Dearborn, just north of the Loop, where the satsang was held. Oddly enough, given my Methodist upbringing, I had been attracted to Radha Swami also. It was as if my Being said once again, "Remember this." The Hindu principles of karma, reincarnation, and taking a human birth to learn and live out karmic lessons that would raise up my soul on my spiritual path, all made sense to me as an explanation for the inequality of life on earth.

There were five of us to be initiated that cold gray winter day in the drab meeting room of the Y. I remember being nervous as we each were given the mantra individually. I hoped I could pronounce the unfamiliar words and then remember them. No one translated their meaning. Then came the instructions. Eat a vegetarian diet, which we had been following for two months prior to this day, abstain from alcohol and drugs, and meditate two and a half hours a day, based on tithing a tenth of your day. Then listen for the sound and watch for the light all emanating from God. Voila! One day it will happen and you will be enlightened. Whatever that meant! The words were magical to me and I repeated them all the way home. But two and a half hours of meditation is hard for anyone to maintain, let alone a novice like me. I struggled with the discipline daily. This was where my idea that meditation was difficult came from, because it was! As a young woman starting my teaching career, I had little time for meditation of that duration, but I repeated my mantra and tried to sit every day. Because I always fell short of the full time, I often felt like a failure. But in my heart and mind I promised myself I would not forget. I would return to a serious practice at some point. I had age fifty in my mind. I guess without being aware of it, I was following the "Grandmother tradition." Many indigenous peoples revere the grandmother as she has earned her time now to pursue spiritual matters.

August 1974, I was preparing my classroom for my fourth year of teaching first grade. I had carefully printed the names from my class list onto Raggedy Ann and Raggedy Andy name tags. I had spent hours tracing, cutting out, and coloring them. All summer Carl and I had been hopeful he would find a teaching position near White Hall. But this was a time of teaching job scarcity, not a teacher shortage. When he was offered a job teaching English at Apollo Junior High in the Chicago suburb of Des Plaines, a part of the large suburban Maine school district, we had no other options. At first we considered my keeping my job, but we soon realized Carl could not make the four hour drive from Chicago every weekend. How often could he make the trip? Reluctantly I resigned and we made the necessary hasty decision to accept the offer and move together. We found an efficiency apartment in a huge complex near the school, got a cat and settled in.

Obviously the only choice in the matter was to be together, but I was heartbroken to be leaving my parents, my hometown, and my church, where I was already taking on my Martha ways, teaching Sunday school, organizing Bible school, and being the local Methodist Women's president. I had naively thought we were settled for life. Thank goodness that wasn't the case!

Now we were able to regularly attend the Radha Swami satsang at the downtown Y every Sunday. The talks were always about "the gist of the teachings." I was able to find the parts of the teachings that were no different than Jesus's teaching. I saw clearly that Jesus had been a perfect master, just not the only one. The comparison actually strengthened my Christian beliefs.

Yet the practices were rule bound and rigid, there was something missing. I didn't know what at the time. At the very least my initiation in Radha Swami was a "remember this" signal from my Being, a very important step on my path. I had a living Master now, but it was physically impossible to be at his feet. Was that what was missing?

Carl continued to seek. We feasted on the spiritual learning opportunities available in the city that we had been missing in rural Illinois. We both saw Ram Dass and Elizabeth Kubler-Ross. Carl saw Swami Satchidananda and attended a Buddhist retreat with Jack Kornfield. His visit to the Chogyam Trungpa center in Chicago was the beginning of Buddhist practice he incorporates in his daily meditation today.

Looking back to that time in the middle and later 70s, we see the foreshadowing of many events that became central to our spiritual development. 'Being' was setting the table. Around that time Carl attended a presentation about the American guru Adi Da at Unity Northwest church in Des Plaines. His attendance at that event was full of "coincidences" that he felt were some kind of spiritual signs. That same church would reappear in our lives. Twenty five years later our daughter became a member of it as a newlywed when she lived in Mount Prospect. Attending the church with her when on visits led us to join the Unity of Fox Valley church after we moved back to the Chicago area to the town of Elburn. And in the 70s and 80s, Carl read all of Adi Da's books and noticed that one of his main devotee-editors was a man named Saniel Bonder. Twenty years later, when Saniel became a teacher himself, Carl recognized his name, and that led us to Saniel's work in Waking Down in Mutuality®.

# CHAPTER 6

# Katie and the Highest Slide

*I* had known I wanted a baby since I was a little girl. Dolls filled my childhood play. A new baby doll was under every Christmas tree. I knew I wanted at least one child. Carl and I both wanted a girl. We neither one wanted to navigate the world of boys, naively thinking a girl would be easier to raise. In truth it is an enormous undertaking no matter the sex. At thirty years old we both were old enough to have made a conscious decision to start a family. Ultrasounds and sex identification in the womb were not standard procedure then. I don't know if I would have chosen to know ahead of time or not. I found it hard to imagine what our baby would be like until I held her in my arms.

Our baby was due August 12, 1977. Labor began on the 13th and Katherine Lee was born at 1:37 a.m. on the 14th, twenty-one hours after the first twinge at 4:30 a.m. the morning before. We were as prepared as was possible for the labor and delivery. We had taken Lamaze classes and were prepared for a natural childbirth. I made it to the transition phase, and then I accepted some Demerol, the effects which put me to sleep and lasted for about two hours. I was in a strange state of being awakened every two minutes as the contractions increased in intensity. As the drug wore off, I then had something else to concentrate on...the pushing. Two and a half hours later Katie arrived. Thank goodness the kind delivery room nurse made sure Carl was with me. I think the old doctor would have ignored my request, even though he knew it was part of the agreement in the Lamaze class. What Dr. Miller lacked in bedside manner, he made up for in skill. He did not interfere in the natural process and indeed complimented me on a job well done the next day. My Lamaze teacher said maybe he would be more open to fathers in the delivery room as a result.

The next day Carl said he felt like he was returning to a battleground as he arrived at the hospital. Later he confided in me that at first he thought he was going to have to follow the circus the rest of his life with a blue pointy headed baby. No one had warned him what a newborn actually looks like!

I enjoyed every stage of Katie's growth. I often mourned the stage just passed. I reluctantly packed away the darling rosebud adorned knit dress, no longer having a precious tiny infant to wear it. Then she went on to walking and talking, with new words every day, after her first words, dada and moo. "Allsly," I finally figured out, was always and usually put together.

"Oh, Katie, why do you always go to the highest slide? Wouldn't you rather swing in the baby swing?"

"Guess not," I thought as she toddled off toward the big ladder. Trips to the park with a two year old should have been easier than this. Kids twice her size and age didn't go near the tall slide. Today the strong-willed determination she exhibited as a child serves her well. She graduated from SIU with majors in marketing and journalism and later became a certified nutritional technician. She is a triathlete, a Dale Carnegie instructor, and has her own nutrition consulting business and works as a diet coach, plus being a wife and mother of two equally energetic children. I often wonder "Where did you come from?" At times as she grew up I felt that she was the mother and I was the child. I didn't push her or hold her back. I allowed her to move at her own pace and to be more outgoing than I was. She definitely was not timid or backwards like I had been.

The next leg of our journey was high on the bluffs overlooking the Mississippi River at Louisiana, Missouri. We had a marvelous southern view of the wide river from our front deck. My fondest memories of our time in Louisiana are of days spent sitting in the porch swing watching the busy barge traffic, recreational boats, and occasionally the Delta Queen riverboat. We moved to this lazy river town because we wanted to get Katie out of the city. Carl began teaching English at the high school there. Louisiana was a cliquish town and we would always be viewed as lesser itinerants. Despite that, I had a small group of good friends. Better yet, now we were just an hour from White Hall – home – and my parents.

Spiritually it became a time to build our inner strength. We did our best to keep the flame of our spiritual motivation alive in a world that wasn't spiritual or mystical. We were in exile. I held lightly to Radha Swami and attended the Methodist church, mainly to take Katie to Sunday school. I meditated sporadically, mostly I focused on raising Katie. I once again promised myself I would return to my spiritual practices at an "easier time." Carl seemed to be on a divergent path from my own. This is when he began to read books by the western spiritual teacher later known as Adi

Da. He also developed an interest in Buddhism. But I didn't have any problem in his pursuing these paths and he started attending Buddhist retreats.

"I'm so happy I could burst!" I thought, as we followed the moving truck to White Hall on a perfect June day in 1984. I was going home, literally, to the house that I grew up in. The previous year dad had had open heart surgery and he wanted to get mother settled in town, in case he was not there to take care of her. He didn't tell her of his fears, but he knew he did not want to leave her alone in the country. After his oldest sister's death the previous fall, they bought her house on Main Street in White Hall and we moved to the farm. They could visit any time they felt homesick for the country. I loved looking up to see Dad pull into the driveway and head to the garden that we tended together. Okra, tomatoes, green beans, corn, I could easily throw together a lunch for the two of us. Mother continued to love flower gardening in her new spacious backyard that also included a quiet timber lot. Happily we had fifteen years of making new and lasting memories in the home in town until their passing.

It seemed normal to resume my "Martha" ways at the church I had left ten years earlier. There were latent forces at work. "Remember this" moments within the walls of this building were ahead of me. The search for

my authentic self had not yet been outwardly precipi-
tated. I needed to "cook" longer. I was drawn to volunteer
to share organist duties with my friend, Ruth. I taught
myself to play the magnificent old pipe organ. My inner
"you could do more" voice prompted me to overcome my
performance anxiety. It took many Sundays for me to
become comfortable, although I always had butterflies in
my stomach every time I switched on that intimidating
instrument, with pipes which filled the front of the
sanctuary. The responsibility was great. As the organist I
set the pace for the service and all eyes were on me. I
could never move to the level of difficulty a trained
musician achieves, but I could produce beautiful music
and play the traditional hymns with few mistakes. I was
happiest practicing alone when I would dare to open all
the stops and let the heavenly sound soar. I felt closest to
God then. Playing the organ became my deepest
meditation. It was a whole body experience that took
focused concentration. My first witnessing experience
happened on that organ bench when I felt at times I was
playing from the lower left side of my body. Often I felt
the ability to play came from outside myself, as if tapping
into another power. I was only able to put words to this
experience after being part of Waking Down in Mutuality
with Saniel Bonder, my future spiritual teacher.

We settled in once again. Carl started teaching at Routt Catholic High School and part time at MacMurray College. He went back to school and graduated with honors from University of Illinois at Springfield with a Masters in counseling and later a third Master's degree in communications. His new profession as a therapist served both his self-understanding and his ability to hold and be compassionate to others. The Buddhist mindfulness qualities he learned through his practice enabled him to listen deeply and understand the suffering of his clients. By listening with calm and understanding, he often eased their suffering.

I wanted Katie to have the opportunity for the same country life experiences I had had growing up, building a lean-to in the timber, learning to ride a bike in our front yard, fishing in the pond, wading in the creek. She had learned to swim in Louisiana and Carl had taken her to the pool every day, so we put up an above ground pool later that summer in time for her birthday. Often she spent afternoons sitting on the huge round hay bales in the west field reading *Anne of Green Gables* or one of the "Little House" books. One afternoon I spied her with a yoke made from an old broom handle across her shoulders with buckets of water on each end. She was acting out the scene in which Laura was trying to save the fruit trees in her new orchard. Her little red sweaty face was set in concentration and effort. She had the typical experiences of any small town girl, piano lessons, little league softball, school dances, cheerleading, mean girlfriends, two very nice boyfriends, and finally, graduation. All passing in a flash. I remember a stranger's words to me at a restaurant, as she smiled at my newborn daughter, "Enjoy every minute with her because before you know it she will be sixteen. My son's age," she added wistfully. Advice I have expressed to every new mother since then.

"I just have to cry," I sniffled as Carl glanced at me. "I know," he agreed. We were returning home after leaving Katie at SIU in Carbondale. The next year, same time, same trip, I was fine. Nothing like having a kid with one year's freedom under her belt to make a mother wish for a short summer! I'm exaggerating, but I wish cell phones had existed that summer. I would have worried less, even though I knew she was working late closing the local Dairy Queen or playing cards with her friends.

Mother talked for weeks about the thick potato soup and warm peach cobbler she relished at our celebration dinner after Katie's college graduation in December 1999. Sadly dad had died in January that year. I am thankful he did get to meet our future son-in-law Keith Nightlinger. One fateful summer day in 1997 as Katie sat on the curb in front of her apartment near campus she noticed a handsome young man as he skated by. Making a U-turn and coming back, he noticed her, too. Katie and Keith were married in June 2000.

Thankfully for me, letting go of my precious daughter followed the natural progression of life.

# CHAPTER 7

# "Insist Persist"

*In* 1990, I returned to teaching as a Title 1 reading teacher. I drove over an hour from White Hall to SIU at Edwardsville to take night classes to earn my reading certification. This was very much out of my comfort zone. My "you could do more" voice was prompting me. I had to use self-talk about staying calm while driving alone, while meeting new people, while learning new material, and being in school once again. While there, I learned about Reading Recovery, a method of teaching struggling first graders to read, developed by Marie Clay in New Zealand. I was intrigued and had wanted to know how children learned to read since teaching first graders twenty years before. When the opportunity to be trained as a Reading Recovery teacher was made available to me, I jumped at the chance.

To say instruction to be an RR teacher was intense is a gross understatement. I see it now as a major growth period for me. A colleague and I made the hour trip to Springfield once a week after school for training. We spent the first part of the five hour class observing two fellow class members teaching a lesson "behind the glass" (BTG) as the teacher leader, Mrs. Eck, led the rest of us in a critique of their teaching. She questioned us continuously as we were trying to observe, so it was nearly as uncomfortable in front of the glass as BTG. The rest of class was spent in instruction. Mrs. Eck was relentless and used the "insist persist" model that we were to use with our students. As hard as it was, I loved it because I did learn how children became readers. All children learn differently, but I was taught how to find the strengths in their process and then teach to those strengths. I developed a great confidence in my teaching. But I never went to class without an angel pin on my lapel. My guardian angel's presence couldn't hurt. I called on her many times.

RR was a new program in the United States. It was expensive to implement in a school district because each teacher had only four students for one-on-one instruction in the afternoon. There was ongoing training the entire time the district was enrolled in the program and we had to follow RR rules about student selection. Illinois was one of the first states to adopt RR after The Ohio State University brought it to the US. Funding was crucial, so our Springfield teaching center was asked to demonstrate the program for the Illinois State School Board. The RR instructors of teacher leaders from the University of Illinois would also be in attendance.

Mrs. Eck asked my colleague and me to teach BTG. I was struck with terror, but also flattered at the confidence she had in our ability to best demonstrate the program. She told us to select one of our students who was making the greatest progress. I picked Joey, the typical little hyper boy, but one who was catching on to the task of reading. All he needed was a dose of Ritalin to help him focus. Mrs. Eck said to be sure and give him a dose right before we left for the hour drive to Springfield.

This is just half of the story.

On the weekend before this event, dad had a problem with his heart and was in St. John's hospital in Springfield. Then in the night, mother had a heart attack at home alone. She did not call me because she knew I had this huge responsibility of teaching BTG later that day. She called a neighbor who got her to the Jerseyville hospital in time. My brother, Bill, who lived in Jerseyville called me early in the morning. Trying his best not to alarm me, told me they would be moving mother to St. John's hospital also.

When I arrived in Springfield with Joey in tow and told Mrs. Eck about my parents, I thought she was going to have a heart attack! She said,"I can't believe I have to ask you to do this now." But we had no choice, all the dignitaries were there.

Later I could see how my mind balanced out the two situations and kept me functioning. As I sat BTG, beyond nervous, trying to think of the next part of the lesson, knowing all eyes were on me, I would think of mom and dad. Then when I would become overwhelmed with fear and concern for my parents, I would have to refocus to be drawn back into the lesson.

What happened next was one of those mystifying occurrences that zap us out of the blue. About twenty minutes into the half hour lesson, during the writing section, little unobservant Joey stopped mid-sentence, turned to me and said, "I like your angel pin." My hand flew to my pin and I thought, "Did he just say that?" I took a breath and said a silent thank you. I knew it was my angel saying, "I'm here, keep going, it will all be okay."

And it was. Joey and I finished the lesson with confidence, mom and dad recovered, Mrs. Eck was thrilled with our teaching, and funding continued for the program.

# CHAPTER 8

# Letting Go

*O*ver time, I have come to realize letting go of attachment is a major step upon the evolutionary path to enlightenment. I naturally grieved and then moved on from major attachments through heartbreaking events that occurred three years before what I call the "chicken pie supper outburst" which I told you about in Chapter 1. I feel very fortunate that I see now how they turned into blessings, allowing me to move on into a greater understanding of the goal. My forgotten knowledge of the infinite reality, oneness with God, beyond what we physically perceive, when we felt part of everything, is what Mary was seeking at the feet of Jesus. Were these the events that started the breakdown of Martha within me?

In early 1994 we started hearing rumors that a mega-factory hog farm corporation wanted to locate down the road within a mile of our home. The fact was, it was more than a rumor; it was a "done deal" by the time we learned of it. But the corporation let us think we still had a say in its establishment. My brother worked tirelessly to find something in the law that would stop it. The closest he came was the land's connection to the Native Americans who had lived there centuries ago. We hoped that their burial grounds would need to be protected, but to no avail. Mother and Dad, Carl and I even took part in a protest walk in front of their headquarters in town. Politicians follow the money, and this was the beginning of my total disillusionment in politics. Especially when our state representative sponsored a family farm day at his father's farm which was downwind of the hog farm. I called him out on his hypocrisy in a letter to the editor in the Springfield newspaper, something I had never dreamed I could have done. We attended hearings and public meetings to express our objections. I could see in the smug expressions of the officials as we spoke, that we were wasting our breath.

Hanor Farms had found their ideal spot, sparsely populated, at the end of a road with very little through traffic. Few people had any reason to be driving near there.

When we were still in the "rumor stage", a friend who usually knew all the local gossip asked me what I knew. From my response she said, "You are in denial." I certainly was, it took me a long time to accept the inevitable.

I remember meeting the front man for the company in my living room with my neighbors. He was a handsome young blond fellow, mild mannered and soft spoken, from Winterset, Iowa. Such a poetic name. What a horrible job, he had to be the first contact with angry and disbelieving people. But he had his spiel down pat. He knew he was breaking our hearts and changing our lives. I almost felt sorry for him. After he left we all sat there stunned, trying to absorb what was going to happen to us. Would we even be able to stay in our homes? Some of the people in the room would be the first to have to move. To its credit, the company bought the homes of my neighbors directly north of the operation; southerly winds made it impossible to tolerate the odors that permeated their homes. I suppose in the long run it saved them a lot of bad publicity.

Around this time I had been feeling so deeply rooted in my home. I had just given a program on "Prairie Smoke" to a local ladies group. I joined Daughters of the American Revolution after mother had done all the research for us to become members. I often thought how my ancestors had lived and walked right where I stood. It was all going to be ruined now. I remember one day walking around my yard howling in anguish and grief.

Construction began late summer, 1995. Katie had left for college and we were in the midst of another teacher's strike, the fourth one in the ten years since we had moved home. Turmoil reigned in my body. I could barely tolerate sitting in union meetings while being encouraged to disrupt the community, all for the lack of some rhetoric on "just cause" omitted from the contract. No one had ever been fired for lack of just cause or even fired period. Although I had been supportive of the union in the past, it was clear to me now that the leadership had become as obstinate as the school board.

One particular day we were squeezed into a room and told we could not leave until our demands had been delivered to the school board. I was in no mood to be ordered about and simply got up and left to sit under a tree. One of my colleagues, a good and kind friend as well, had been sent out, or perhaps had volunteered to come and check to make sure I was not calling the school board with inside information. REALLY! I vowed then to go home and not return until all was settled. The pain of that day is etched in my memory as I cried bitter, sad tears on my drive home, grieving the loss of my home as I knew it, missing Katie, and now feeling the alienation of my closest friends. But as wrenching as speaking up had been for me, I could not go along with what felt so wrong in my heart. The community did not deserve to go through this again. Extremes on both sides had taken over and were locked in a no win battle, leaving those in the middle silent. So I went home.

As I drove home that day, I followed a semi, loaded with the concrete slats used on the floors of the confinement buildings where the hogs' manure would drop through into the system to be flushed into the massive lagoons. The reality set in that over 80,000 hogs were going to be within a mile of my home and there was nothing I could do about it. The whole operation covered hundreds of acres. There were eight sites, each with eight confinement buildings, each building holding 1100 hogs. The buildings were set near a lagoon the size of three football fields. The waste from each lagoon was sprayed onto acres of alfalfa fields that surrounded each site. Multiply that by eight.

Traffic increased on our once quiet country road. Semi-trucks loaded with feed roared by all day. Semi-trailers full of finishing sized hogs arrived daily since the pigs were not born near us, but at another location. The UPS truck made twice daily deliveries of antibiotics and hormones. The "dead wagon" was the most frequent vehicle I saw, with numerous trips a day to dump the carcasses at a refrigerated building on the other side of town until the dog food company took them away. Hogs are easily stressed. A high percentage of them die in confinement. But the worst of the traffic came at around 4:00 a.m., when the semis loaded with hogs headed for slaughter would drag by. I often woke to their screams as they were packed so tightly together that they easily crushed each other. I could not allow myself to dwell on this cruelty along with everything else already breaking my heart.

We learned to live with the putrid odors. We were "lucky" to live west of the farm, since most winds blew the worst of the odors to the north or east. On occasion, easterly winds blew in our direction and all windows would have to be closed tightly and no laundry would be put out on those days. Every day as I left for school, however, I was met with the smell as it hung on the heavy morning air. It is a smell you never get used to.

If I had not understood it fully before, I knew it now. Life is change and I would have to let go. I had, indeed, been "blasted" out of my attachment to my home. There was little solace for me in my church community either. Most were not sympathetic. I stopped going to my adult

Sunday school class when the hog farm, seen as progress for our community, became a topic for discussion. I had to face the fact that there were those there that I had known and loved who were not on my side. The seed of breaking another major attachment was taking root. I was being "blasted" out of this attachment to my church, as well. What they saw as progress, more money for the school district and more jobs for our depressed area, I saw as the ugly truth that we need only "follow the money " to see the worth and word of our politicians and even our friends and neighbors. The truth is agricultural endeavors are tax exempt for many years. There were not that many jobs involved. I saw mostly strangers doing the construction. One of the highest paying jobs was given to the son-in-law of one of the land sellers. I called it manure manager. How appropriate! I see now who the losers were. These people had chosen money over friendship or family or community affiliation. My prayer is that they have healed as well as I have.

At the time, I turned to affirmations I found in *Simple Abundance*, by Sarah Ban Breathnach, and my angel cards. I was drawn into the daily anecdotes of comforting acts and self-care. I discovered that many days the messages resonated with my soul. The dig to find me, the authentic me, was begun with my discovery of this book and my angel cards. My true authoritative self was buried deep. Is she calling? Will I hear her? Will I get the message and then heed it?

I drew the angel card "JOY" on one particular day. It was to be my twenty-first day of walking the picket line. "Joy is the natural state of the spiritually-ordered person. Joy is the inner understanding that all things are held in loving embrace of God and the angels and that a meaningful explanation and learning will emerge that will ultimately benefit us all. Life can offer you no inner peace until you determine to accept it for yourself. Tomorrow will be no different from today. Rather than remaining hostage to life's changes, expect understanding and continued Joy to flow to you and it will." How will I feel this Joy? What will take me out of this situation? On this day I didn't know, but I wrote "Joy" on a scrap of paper and put it in the pocket of my jeans. When I was tempted to despair I would touch the paper and just concentrate on my next step down the sidewalk.

It was two days later that I was involved in the terrible scene at the union meeting when I had walked out. This joy of the authoritative-self, I could see, was going to come with a price. My heart will hold my feet to the alchemist's fire, where we are tested and transformed into our higher-self. That was the day that I decided to follow my heart and cross the picket line with a handful of colleagues and the support of the community and an organized group of determined parents. I was going to test my voice in a major way. Couldn't I have chosen something less dramatic? My Being said, "No!"

On the thirty-sixth day of the strike, approximately twenty-five teachers and seventy substitutes crossed the picket line. I had never felt as heartsick as I did that chilly late October day. Carl drove me to the farm pasture on the edge of town, where we "scabs" met to go in together on buses. The substitutes from far and wide needed a secure place to leave their cars. A wave of nausea hit me when I saw State Police cars lining the road. Carl reassured me that I was doing the right thing. Women with whom I had taught for years were posted at the driveway of the home screaming at us and videotaping our arrival. As we sat on the bus we were mostly silent, each feeling the enormity of what we had chosen to do. There were more taunts as we departed; we just looked at each other and shook our heads. Who had these people become, chanting, red-faced and bullying us? The negative shadow had arisen so quickly in these people, people I otherwise knew to be excellent educators and dedicated to their profession. Their anger, fear, and disbelief at our "disloyalty" overcame them. Their fear stemmed from their underestimation of the determination of the parents to restore their children's education. There was a faction of teachers who had bragged about shutting down the school for all year.

There were more police at the school to clear the entrance to the drive. Thankfully, the buses pulled around to the back of the building where the picketers could not see us unload. The sounds of excited cheering children began to drown out the jeering crowd outside as we entered the gym. The principal greeted us with tears in her eyes, and a heartfelt welcome speech. Parents thanked us personally. Later I received many notes of gratitude from the community. I certainly didn't feel like a hero that day, but we did our best to settle the students and ignore the chaos of the situation.

The union knew they were defeated because we persevered despite their efforts to disrupt the day by sending in their spouses to observe and check the credentials of the subs. I followed one particular reporter who was looking for a story, to make sure what he reported was the truth. I found it disturbing that he went into the loudest classroom to fluster the sub, while right next door the class was already settled and working. I asked one of the fathers to escort him out. He got this "What? Who me?" innocent look on his face, but I knew better. I knew the teachers had sent him to this particular lady's room. I spent the day locating teacher's manuals buried in the rooms. Materials were hidden in black plastic bags stuffed on top of storage cabinets. The refrigerator from the teacher's lounge had been removed. The childish revengeful tactics they had sunk to were astounding.

I have long ago forgiven them, but their actions are hard to forget. Yet another attachment had been broken. My friends, colleagues, and the job itself no longer felt the same to me. I let go of my identification with the childhood dream of being the perfect teacher.

A week later the teachers returned and I literally was detached. I went into my room and kept my contact with them minimal and professional. The ugliness, bitterness, and frustration eventually healed, as much as possible. Before retiring ten years later, I felt accepted by most everyone again.

This period of my life was unleashing the qualities of an authentic woman that I had been hiding all my life, testing me at every turn. I needed to find my voice and speak without guilt. I could no longer hide my courage or my anger, and above all I needed to learn to let go. I could have become stuck in bitterness and revenge about my changing home, church, friends, and profession. But I see now these were my toughest attachments to break, crucial to seeing the larger picture of oneness. When I view non-reaction from the perspective of multiple lifetimes, I see how insignificant one incident is, even the most challenging one. How do we treat people? Do my actions hurt or help others on their journey or me on mine? What lessons have I set out to learn in this lifetime? My judging is futile when viewing the karmic past actions of relationships with others. Today it is a relief to feel the insignificance of all these seemingly monumental events. At the time, I did not recognize the hints of self-empowerment. Yet self-empowerment is the gateway to overcoming numbness and expanding Joy. I found I became more compassionate with my students. Sarah was one such student.

# CHAPTER 9

# Sarah

*Most* often, the children I worked with had far greater problems than delayed progress in reading. The heap of mental abuse and poverty these little ones faced before walking through our doors at 8:00 a.m. would have been a challenge for most adults. Kindergartener Sarah was a cute blonde with brown eyes and freckles across her nose. She was big for her age. She had poor verbal skills, but enough to be disruptive in class. Her older brother had been in special education for years and her parents refused, at first, to send Sarah down the same path. Every day I would see her sitting outside her classroom, separated from the class. Usually the teacher's aide would be with her, drilling her on phonics skills.

Something about the spark in her eyes broke my heart. She didn't really have a sad look nor a defiant one, just a confused one, asking why. She covered her sadness well.

When she became my student, I made accommodations for her, letting her move around when she needed. She would often refuse to do what the other children were doing, so I let her draw. She was good at that. I decided to work with her alone during my own scheduled break time. Soon she began to read.

The week prior to St. Patrick's Day, all three classrooms of kindergarteners had been "trying to trap a leprechaun" in their homemade traps. Each wanted to be the one who caught that pesky elf. Each morning we could hear their excitement from down the hall, discovering traces of his glittered footprints around the classroom, even on the ceiling. Each day he had escaped their traps and evidence of his presence was found in another corner of the room. By the end of the week every kindergartener was whipped into a frenzy of excitement. The culmination of the week would be a party when the children would find the leprechaun on a beautifully decorated cake.

Every kindergartener except Sarah, that is. I was heartbroken to look down the hall and see her once again, sitting outside the classroom door while inside the other children were laughing and playing. What could she have done to deserve this? Without thinking, I marched down the hallway and told her we would have a party of our own. I caught the eye of the teacher's aide in the room and indicated I was taking Sarah with me. She nodded with a grateful knowing look.

I fought back tears as I asked her to wait for me outside the teacher's lounge while I searched in the freezer for some ice cream I had seen earlier. When I emerged with the ice cream, the janitor was chatting with Sarah. He had seen her earlier sitting in the hall. "That wasn't right, was it?" he said to me. "I'm glad you took her." He said he admired my nerve. I wasn't worried about what her teacher would say at that point. I knew in my heart her reason for excluding Sarah could not be better than mine for stepping in. Maybe she was happy I stepped in. She never said anything about the incident and neither did I.

We quietly ate the ice cream and colored pictures. Neither of us said a word about what was happening down the hall. Much later, the aide came to the door and asked Sarah if she would like to return to the room for some cake. She nodded her head yes.

A year later, Sarah's parents agreed to testing and a special education placement. I was so relieved when I

Lucy Jane Strang
4-5 years old

Lucy Jane Strang
1st Grade

Lucy & Carl Klemarier, Married Sept. 4, 1971

Lucy & Katie
1977

Lucy & Carl,
Kate & Ketih Nightlinger,
Brady & Annelise
2010

William H. Strang
Lura Lee Strang

heard her new teacher would be a kind young woman, the mother of one of my former students. The smaller class, and one-on-one instruction, proved to be the best solution for Sarah.

Through the years, I had seen other students treated this way, but had never intervened. But as my heart opened through my spiritual work, I found my compassion increased and also my courage. I came to understand that the children I worked with were baby souls on their own journeys, with karmic lessons of their own. My job was to be compassionate and love them as best as I could.

# CHAPTER 10

# An Honorable Man

On Sunday, January 23, 1999, as I sat in the Memorial Hospital lounge, in Springfield, I was facing another life changing transition. The second floor oncology ward had the kindest personnel I had ever encountered. The nurses did not hesitate to ensure dad was comfortable and pain free. We had moved dad from Jersey County Community Hospital on Friday morning. That evening as the doctor looked at dad's chest X-ray, he gently said to him, "You don't complain much do you?" He was shocked to find one lung almost completely filled with fluid. He did not wait for an operating room to become available, but decided to start the drain immediately, in his room. The official cancer diagnosis was not made until the test results came on Monday after dad passed away on Sunday night at 10:25 p.m. Carl and I made the decision to take mother home Sunday evening. She was exhausted and disoriented; not herself. She agreed that she wanted to go home. My sister Mary Lee and her husband Jerry, and my brother Bill and his wife Gloria stayed with dad. I can still picture the rosy red and purplish streaked sunset that filled the western sky as we drove home. I knew dad would not be here much longer. I don't recall mother saying anything. Dad had been sick since Christmas and it had taken a toll on her physically and mentally. His illness marked the beginning of her decline.

After we got mother settled at her house, we went home. I remember feeling how different everything around me seemed, as we pulled into the drive. I sat in the car as my tears fell, knowing that dad would not ever see his birth place again. I knew my mind and body would not relax enough to sleep without a pill. So I took a whole sleeping pill, enough to knock me out all night, yet in a half hour I awoke crying. It was 10:25 p.m. I knew dad was gone before the phone rang ten minutes later when Bill called to tell me dad had passed.

At 88 years old, dad had lived a long and honorable life. He was well respected and a responsible community member. He served in leadership positions on the school board, church board, Coop Elevator board, Farm Bureau, 4-H, Masons, Lions Club, Meals-on-Wheels. He was a dutiful Martha, too. Fifty somber Masons in their aprons performed the last rites ritual in an impressive ceremony after 300 townspeople had attended the visitation. The next day the church sanctuary was full. The service and eulogies were comforting. The funeral dinner was bountiful and lovingly served by all the church ladies.

Dad was a father to be proud of. And I always had been. I have examined our relationship in many group sessions on Waking Down retreats. After coming to know myself better, I traced my lack of confidence in speaking with men to our silence with each other. He taught by example, not words. In fact, I cannot recall one conversation when he ever said what I should do or how I should act. The truth is, I didn't know what he was thinking, his inner workings, his griefs, or his triumphs. All was a mystery to me. I longed for a closer relationship with him. My shyness and hiding away stemmed from his taciturn personality and putting up with very little foolishness. Over time and reflection I realized the strength of our relationship was the trust I had in him as the stable solid background of my life. He was the same every day. He was not moody. I knew exactly what to expect from him. I felt safe when he was near and knew that he could take care of any situation that might arise. I knew this intellectually, but feeling that knowledge and letting go of the pain is different.

Many years later, in a Waking Down weekend in our home in Elburn with Fax and Sharon Gilbert, I experienced the final resolution of my conflicting feelings about my relationship with dad. Fax asked us to reflect upon our strongest authentic traits. First I told them what Allen Morelock, a psychically gifted Waking Down teacher, had told me in a reading of my name, at our first transfiguration retreat. Lucy means lucid, light; Jane means plain, ordinary; and Strang means strong. All these traits reflected in my name were a good omen for my further growth and evolution into awakening.

"I'm responsible, honest, hardworking, quiet, and trustworthy. I think I'm a good wife, mother, and grandmother. I was a good and caring teacher."

Fax said, "And where do you think those qualities came from?"

"My dad," I whispered through my tears. In that moment the bubble of confusion surrounding our relationship burst. Knowing that my finest strongest qualities came from him, erased forever my sad feelings about us. One of the fellow retreat participants pointed out, "He was an honorable man." No child could ask for a better description of their father.

I should have also added dad's capacity to forgive to his list of qualities. With one act of forgiveness, he broke a karmic cycle of pain that had probably been passed generation to generation.

With the death of my grandfather in 1960, came the heartache of betrayal fueled by greed that often happens in families when inheritances are at stake. The will said, 'share and share alike'. The numbers in dollars and acres look small in comparison to today, but then they were significant. Dad wanted to buy his sisters' shares of the farm at a fair price that he felt he could afford. Three of his sisters wanted more. One sister said she would sell her share at dad's price.

"None of us would have anything to sell if not for William," she pointed out. During the depression, dad worked his own rental ground to make ends meet and then helped his dad late into the night, for no pay. Somehow they were able to hang onto the land and keep it from bank foreclosure as they saw many neighbors losing their farms. In a meeting with an official of the Franklin Life Insurance Company which had bought their taxes, mother and dad were shocked to learn that unbeknownst to them, my grandfather had named them as grantees in a quitclaim deed. This placed all the responsibility of debt on them without guarantee of future ownership. My Aunt Babe who understood all this said to the other three, "Mom and Dad would not want you to treat William this way."

"They're dead, they won't know," the youngest sister replied.

Mother and dad decided not to go into debt for land he had already paid for in sweat and toil. As they sat in the lawyer's office reading the will, mother told the sisters, "We would rather spend the money to educate our children." Mary Lee chose business school, I graduated debt free from EIU, and Bill received his law degree from Washington University in St. Louis. After Bill graduated, mother and dad gave Mary Lee and I each a check to help make up for the differences in the costs of our schooling. Their fairness and generosity is reflected in how we treat each other to this day.

Mother shed many bitter tears over the injustice and greed of dad's sisters, but I never heard dad say one word. I'm sure he and mother discussed the situation, but behind closed doors. One cold snowy day the surveyor came to mark off the land sold to a neighbor, mother looked out the picture window and saw dad's oldest and youngest sisters tromping around in the frozen cornstalks watching the procedure. They acted as if they needed to supervise, to ensure the neighbor would get every last square inch of land due him. I was in junior high by this time and old enough to feel my parents' pain. On this day when I arrived home I knew something very hurtful had happened. Shortly after mother started having terrible dreams. She soon realized she and dad must put their grief behind them or it would destroy their life and health.

Several years passed and we had little contact with these aunts. We didn't dwell on the separation. Then in the early 1970's my oldest aunt's husband died. I remember discussion about whether or not we would acknowledge his death or attend the visitation and funeral. Dad made the decision to go. Mother told me how hard it had been to walk up the sidewalk and onto the porch of my aunt's house. When my aunt answered the door and saw dad, she broke down in tears and they held out their arms to each other. "Oh you came," she cried.

His soul had taken a step up.

Recently I was reading about a character in a story helping another character remove his boots. Suddenly a calm, loving feeling came into my heart as a childhood memory of helping dad take off his old worn work shoes flashed in my mind. "Janie, take off my shoes." I loved that he was the only one who called me Janie. I would sit at his feet and slowly unwind the laces first from the hooks and then loosen them enough to pull off the shoes. As this sweet moment came floating back into my memory, I began to think of other times of quiet companionship we had shared. I often went with him to do the evening chores, feeding the hogs and cattle. Sometimes my brother Bill went too. I would watch Dad scoop the golden corn into the troughs, put out hay for the cows, and slop the hogs. Bill and I played in the cattle shoot or climbed on the fences pretending we were on horseback. As the sun was setting, we would return to the warm kitchen for a supper of sausage, mashed potatoes, and bread and gravy. Bill and I would chatter about our day as mom and dad listened. I don't ever want to forget the blessings of an ordinary life.

# CHAPTER 11

## Lura's Light

She left before the Autumn Light,
'Tho that be how she's captured
Inside this mind's photography.

Out on that good and golden prairie…
Reigning victorious 'mongst blooming rapture,
Stood Nature's Queen, jeweled in earth's crust.
Tattered and windblown, Vanity deferred
Hark…Time…the halted school bus!

Two small girls with artwork fast gathered,
Compete to be first a galloping must.
As they giggle and gossip, they're sunned by her grin.

Talking and shouting, won't stir up the dust,
And they dance 'round her skirts on their way in.
A swift pause in the chatter, a glance up at her face,
Yet to show wrinkle or be framed in white,
Still see her freeze-framed 'neath a tree of
leafed lace,
All sprinkled with glitter of Autumn's
Sweet Light

Softly, gentle ladies, in the bedroom that night,
Locked in age old rituals requiring imagination,
Not a bit peculiar to any generation or race,
Dressed dollies and doted in blind concentration.
A glance up towards the door revealed her in
that place.
"Oh, my, each of your babies has such a good
mother!"
A precious compliment stored back for solace,
or laugh!
This one misses the gathering of those familiar.
Yet, does take this advantage of solitude hush,
To reflect on a life of a woman,
Who has momentarily left us.
Her essence forthcoming in refreshing wind,
Transcending to sparkle of Sweet Autumn Light!

This precious gift of a poem was written by Suzie Frioli, my first best friend, for my mother, Lura Lee Lorton Strang. In first grade, Suzie and I sat across the aisle of bolted down school desks from each other. This poem is a recollection of one of our many overnights. She captured mother's loving kindness perfectly. One of my favorite lines is "Tattered and windblown, Vanity deferred." Mother did not care about her appearance when she was at work in her blooming flowerbeds.

My heart broke to watch her rapid physical and mental decline after dad's death. I checked on her every day on my way home from school. One day as soon as I opened the back door I knew something was terribly wrong. She had fallen into the dry bathtub and hadn't had the strength to climb out. She had been there all night and all day. Her time of living at home alone was over.

For a woman who had spent most of her life in the solitude of the country and the beauty of her quiet, tree lined yard, living with others was difficult. I mourned for the mother I had known. Her caregivers and fellow residents would never know the lovely, generous, and kind woman she truly was. She became angry and at times uncooperative. Many times on my daily visits after school, I would find her sitting at the dining table staring at her uneaten lunch. She was wasting away.

Her decline was the only thing that made it easier to let her go.

On the last Monday in August 2001, I was not surprised when Brenda, the owner of the assisted living facility, called to ask me to move mother to a nursing home. "I cannot watch your mother die." She had cared for her for eighteen months and she knew the end was near.

That Wednesday my sister-in-law, Gloria, helped me move mother to a nursing home in Jerseyville. Gloria did her best to keep the conversation light and cheerful, but our hearts were heavy as we drove her past her home for the last time. On Friday, right after lunch, she died. It was August 31, 2001, shortly before the atrocities of 9-11. I was grateful she never knew about that. I was comforted by the words of the wife of one of her tablemates who came each meal to help feed her Alzheimer's-stricken husband. "I was so shocked to hear your mother had died when I returned for supper. We had visited at lunch. I would have even called her 'animated.' " There was comfort in knowing she had simply left the lunch table for her afternoon nap and passed quietly in her sleep.

The next morning I slowly climbed the back stairs to the church sanctuary. I needed to choose the music for the funeral. I turned on the old pipe organ, coupled the keyboards, and opened the songbook, when a note started to play softly at first and then louder. Thinking the key was stuck, I tapped underneath the keyboards, as I usually did, to remedy the problem. But the high note continued. I started to play, thinking I might hit the right note and it would stop, but it persisted. The key seemed dead as I located the note. (Later I tested it and it was not dead.)

"OK, Mother, I know you are here." I sat and cried as I listened for the longest time. I finally had to turn off the organ to quiet the note. To follow our theme of 'love' for the funeral, I chose "The Power of Your Love" as the solo for my friend Cindy to sing. My sister Mary Lee's eulogy "I Loved You Best" typified mother's greatest gift as a parent. She loved each one of us best and equally.

The next week after the funeral my sister and I started to sort out the house when I found a picture album of Christmas 1997, 1998, and 1999. There was a picture of Katie, Keith, Carl, and me standing over the stove in my kitchen, admiring the golden brown turkey, except I have been meticulously cut out of the picture. Mary Lee was sad that I thought Mother in her dementia had been upset with me and cut me out on purpose. "You know Mother loved you." Yes. I knew.

The next day as we continued our cleaning, Mary Lee said, "Before we get started, I want to show you something mother wrote about you and we're going to paste it over that hole in the picture." She had written on a small scrap of paper, "Devoted her life to Carl, Katie, her parents, and the church, and a great love for her position as a teacher." I don't know when or why she had written it.

As we were going through Christmas ornaments we thought it would be nice to give some of the ones she got for her 75th birthday to the people who had given them to her as a remembrance. Most were labeled, but we had a question about a couple of them. I knew she had a list of them in a scrapbook, so we went to the den to look. We looked through two or three books. Then I saw it, my cutout picture. I gasped, "There it is! I knew it had to be here somewhere." My sister grabbed me and we sobbed. After we cried awhile, I looked closer at the page. This scrapbook was not like her usually well-organized ones. She had obviously put this one together after dad's death. There was an odd combination of pictures on the page, one of my nephews Will and Dan with Katie when they were small, next to information about Tennessee, next to a Super Bowl schedule. In the center of the page next to my cutout was a note from the church newsletter that I had written to thank the congregation for an azalea I had received for being the organist. It read:

Dear Church Family,

Thank you so much for the beautiful azalea. It will brighten my living room the rest of the winter.

Playing our organ is a joy to me. It lifts my spirits to hear that beautiful sound.

Love, Lucy

Then I thought of that one single note that mother played for me, that one "beautiful sound."

I had only one lucid dream when I felt mother's presence. In the dream I was going down a crowded escalator in a train station, when I spotted mother in front of me. She was wearing the light olive green wool coat I had helped her select the previous winter. The coat was so petite. She had gotten smaller and smaller as she aged. In the dream she was checking the train schedule board near the tracks. As I approached her, she turned and smiled. "What does this little angel want?" she asked.

"I want my mother," I sobbed. I awoke in tears. I feel solace now fifteen years later, knowing she was boarding the train to her next destination.

# CHAPTER 12

# Remember This?

*A*fter my parents' deaths, my life settled into a comfortable, but boring routine. Without the responsibility and concern for their care, I was free to move on. Each day was the same, living without effort, teaching school, and doing my church work. But then I began to hear that nagging insistent voice, "You could do more. There's more. You don't have to be numb. The mundane busyness of life is consuming you." It was time to fulfill the promise I had made to myself decades before, that I would return to my spiritual pursuit which I knew was the key to becoming Mary.

Was it a curse or a blessing…being a late bloomer… being ordinary…living a normal life? I see that it enabled me to prepare for the next phase, to move from Martha and into a greater understanding of what it might take to be Mary. Now I know it is the ongoing integration of both that is necessary to carry our empowerment into the world. But in 2002, I just knew the path awaited me.

When mother took me to Sunday school at age five, I developed a love for that church. Jesus was love to me. My Being said, "Remember this? Go on, live this, serve here, grow and worship here." My Being protected me from negative indoctrination. My love of Spirit seen through the teachings of Jesus, developed with lessons learned about how to live and be a "good" person.

In the middle of this time of church and Jesus also came Radha Swami. My Being said again, "Remember this? These are the Hindu principles." I readily accepted the principles of karma and reincarnation with lifetimes of lessons to be learned as we uncover the Divine truth of our Being. This was my allotted time to learn how to become authentic, a time to test my reactions, to realize my strengths and overcome my weaknesses. I would call it the alchemy of life. So it was at age fifty that the essays on living an authentic life and digging for the "real you" in *Simple Abundance* began to resonate inside me and rekindle my search upon my path. Then came Saniel Bonder and Waking Down in Mutuality™. Being didn't just say, "Remember this?" It said, "Here it is!"

One spring day in 2002, Carl came into the kitchen holding *What Is Enlightenment? magazine.* He showed me an ad for a retreat in Boulder, Colorado. "This guy wrote Adi Da's biography, and was his devotee for twenty years. I think I'll go check him out. Do you want to go, too?"

"No, but you can go and see what you think." I had never been able to read more than a few pages of Adi Da's work. But I encouraged him to go because I knew he was still in search of a greater enlightened experience.

He called me from the road on his return home across Kansas. "Luce, something's happening, I'm laughing and crying. I don't know why! I think I've been blasted with transmission!"

"What do you mean by that?" I asked.

"You know, an activation of an awareness of spiritual energy beyond the ordinary." He later told me that when Ben Hurst, the teacher of his small group, stood up and said everyone there deserved to be awakened, he had felt physically blasted in his chest and his whole body had been pushed back.

I was intrigued. I decided to take the recommended Human Sun Seminar on the phone. I understood parts of the teachings, but some of the terms seemed very intellectual and abstract. What did greenlighting, landing platform, witnessing mean? Yet I didn't reject the idea of going deeper.

Hadn't I been seeking and meditating for thirty years? Here's the seminar question that hooked me. "If this was you for eternity would it be OK?" No, it would not be OK. I knew there was more, much more. Who am I?

On a beautiful Friday afternoon in October 2002, I hurriedly met Carl after school. We followed the Great River Road north to cross the Mississippi River at Keokuk on our way to Fairfield, Iowa. We couldn't believe our good fortune that my first Waking Down retreat was within driving distance. The first of many wonderful weekends spent in Fairfield, the home of Maharishi University of Management. Most of the attendees were long time TM (Transcendental Meditation) practitioners. We met in a *vastu* architectural design country home off the grid. The cosmic harmony and support of the structure provided a special atmosphere that even I could sense.

It was not love at first sight. All the first time experiences made me uncomfortable. Gazing, just what it says, looking into the eyes of the teacher for several minutes, made me extremely nervous. I couldn't concentrate on anything except holding the gaze when my first instinct was to look away. I had never been so intensely "seen." The afternoons were spent in small groups of five participants with a teacher where we shared our thoughts and experiences for twenty-five minutes.

What was I going to talk about for that long? Somehow I filled the time as the teacher, Van Nguyen, led me along. I was hesitant to speak about my Christian background among the group of TM people with long histories of meditation and transcendent experiences. I imagined they were much more enlightened than I was. At the time I did not have my "voice", but Van was so kind and drew out of me what spiritual qualities of my faith I understood. He compared God with the ocean of consciousness and I was a wave in that ocean and always a part of that. I left feeling compelled to continue. I didn't quite know why.

At this first retreat during a creative sharing evening, Geoffrey Oelsner read his poem, "Shiver of Light."

Shiver of light
jolts the winter star-points.
I shake a little round my spinal axis.
Without a body to be cold in,
could I love those sparrows?
Without our ribbed existence here,
no tender hearts in cages.
Once there was no shiver,
just UNCARVED BLOCK.
Once there was no tremor,
nor shimmer. Once there were

no ears, and so no songs,
nor silence. But tonite,
I stand by the sparrows.

I was strangely touched by this poem. I became aware of the importance of my aliveness. Only in being alive was I going to get in touch with All. What did that even mean to me? As we drove home the sight of flocks of birds gathered to fly south for the winter brought me to tears. Why did I get that poem? I didn't know, but I felt oddly and unfamiliarly open in my chest.

I had a renewed interest in spiritual reading and found signs in everything I read. Melody Beattie's book, *Journey into the Heart,* inspired me at the beginning of my Waking Down path. When I became discouraged I reread her reassuring quotes that upheld my faith that I was on the right path.

"Trust the rhythm of the universe. You are right where you need to be. You'll get where you need to go. You have all the time you need."

"You may have begun a time of deep transformation, a journey chosen by your soul. Feel all you need to feel. Allow thoughts to flow. Let your body shift. Let yourself be transformed."

I realized I had sat in silence in church long enough. Every Sunday was like the last. It had been four years since my initial outburst of frustration at the chicken pie supper. Nothing had changed. I was the only one who could bring more conscious awareness and awakening into my life. Waking Down calls the breaking down of old ways of fixing discontent the "rot." In retrospect I discovered that Sarah Ban Breathnach, in *Simple Abundance,* had described it as Divine Discontent. She calls it the "grit in the oyster before the pearl." You feel a dissatisfaction about things that used to serve you, make you happy. The euphoric feeling that I had felt at first in Waking Down started to disappear and certainly I hadn't felt satisfied in my faith a long time before that. My "rot" looked like the "blahs." Numbness had been my companion for so long I didn't recognize it as anything, but normal. Ban Breathnach quotes English historian Dame Wedgwood, "Discontent and disorder are signs of energy and hope, not despair. It is part of the process when we are able to grasp the power necessary to open ourselves to the Divine."

During this time I read Saniel's *Conscious Principle* paragraph by paragraph, trusting that what he said was true, the transmission is in the reading of it. In my journal I wrote line after line, to seek clarification from Carl later and then further discuss each question with my first Waking Down in Mutuality mentor, Karen Steen. We talked about my frustration with the feeling "I don't get it" during every phone session. She was always so good at pointing out what I did get. Even with all my questions I did understand that the White-Hot Yoga of the Heart was Saniel's transmission of energy and power needed for transformation. During an especially frustrating time of uncertainty, my dreams answered my questions, too. In one dream I was sitting at the organ fumbling with my music trying to find the right page. My faceless teacher, sitting to the right of me, handed me the music inside a folded magazine. There was no stand to hold the music. The music was indecipherable with symbols, notes, letters, and numbers all over the page. But I started playing anyway, quite a complicated piece. My hands flew up and down the keyboard.

"I played that fairly well," l thought. Afterward I asked Carl, "How did I do?"

"Just fine."

In April 2003, I sat in another small group led by Van. I was the only woman in the group. The Saturday afternoon sharing was not very satisfying. I felt put off and forced into my insecurities. I felt I was only there because of Carl. I thought that's what the group thought, too. What did I expect awakened life to be like? It was a difficult concept for me to grasp. Then on Sunday I was last to speak. I talked about the struggles my students had in reading and how most had such sad lives and lived in poverty. Van then spoke the words that became my turning point, my impetus to persevere. "You are an old soul. The children you work with are baby souls. Your job is to give them love."

"Well, even if I am just here because of Carl, I need to know what this is all about."

"No," Van said, "you are here for yourself."

That was the moment I realized that I, too, could experience a Second Birth, the term Saniel uses to describe the awakening to our conscious nature.

Once again the pressure was on when I would meet Saniel in person for the first time. A large enough group had been established in Fairfield that Saniel and his partner, Linda Groves-Bonder made the trip from their home in California to conduct the retreat. (Years later, Linda became known by many as Linda Ma. That's how I most often refer to her.)

I still agonized over my extended sharing times. Sharing broke all my rules of keeping quiet until I knew for sure of the answer to avoid being negatively judged. As others shared their stories of fear and grief, many with shattered lives they were dealing with, what Saniel termed "broken zones," I began to realize I had actually had a charmed life. Then I began to worry about not having any core issues. Soon it was my turn and I shared about my background and how my seeking was less intense than Carl's. I related about the different philosophies Carl had explored that I didn't always pursue myself. I talked about all the books Carl read that I found too difficult and had no interest in. We laughed about how many "eyes glaze over" moments I had endured through the years, all the while trying to appear interested, as Carl would read paragraph after paragraph of Buddhist teaching. Yet I heard something in Waking Down that struck a chord within me.

"He's finally brought you something you can use!" Indeed, that was exactly how I felt. Saniel said to me, "My sense is that you two made a soul's covenant agreement before entering this lifetime to awaken together. Rely on him." He went on. "You haven't thought this was possible for you. I'm telling you it is! You don't need to have read all those shelves of books."

Saniel's advice to me was to focus a little each day on what and where consciousness was. I continued to study *The Conscious Principle* and feel the sense of expanded energy I felt in meditation. Discernment increased steadily, but it would be eight years before I would own my truth and claim a second birth awakening.

Through the years I often found that on the second day of those weekend retreats, I would feel let down, excluded, dumb, inarticulate, exposed, not quite up to it, separate, and rejected. I would search for the place I felt rejected, but I couldn't find it because I hadn't really been rejected. The feeling came more from being forced out of my comfort zone. I was used to feeling competent and in control. People around me usually looked to me. They noticed what I ate, what my views were, how I taught, what I read. Yet there in those retreats I felt dumb.

Then I had the insight about myself of "being one of the best." There have been very few times in my life when I wasn't one of the best. Early on in my first encounters with other children, like in first grade when I confused six and seven, I knew I didn't want to feel dumb. Where had this "being one of the best" attitude come from? I characterized myself as a shy child, but perhaps a better description would be reserved and quiet. My pattern from the beginning was keep quiet until I knew for sure. This was true in all things, how to sing, how to answer, and how to interact. I was a back row person, always saying to myself, don't reveal your ignorance, don't ask any dumb questions, and don't try to sing until you know you can. I wanted to be the best because being the best meant approval. So I covered up my authentic self and took on

"I'm shy. Don't judge me. I'm going to sit here in my quiet shyness and figure this out on my own. I won't offer a response until I'm sure of the answer. Then you can't judge me."

In sharing this insight with my mentor, Karen, she told me to own my intelligence. I needed to think back on my strengths and let them fuel me. "Your little kid is popping up! Give her a voice. Feel the anxiety, then let it go." This is the wisdom of Linda Groves-Bonder's six step yoga of recognition. See it, feel it, live it, be it, transcend it in place, speak it at appropriate moments along the way.

In 2004, Carl and I made our first trip to California to attend a Waking Down transfiguration retreat. Negotiating San Francisco airport was a nerve-wracking experience for two rural Illinois country folk, but after making a few wrong turns and an unexpected drive to Petaluma we got headed back toward the ocean and located the Marconi Conference Center at Tamales Bay. I wondered if I would have the breakthrough I longed for during this week of intense exposure in this awakened setting.

On the first night as Saniel talked about his journey and his work, my mind raced to take it all in. The clearest message I received that opening night was that most people have a second birth experience within two years of being in the work. Then Saniel began to gently tease a man in the front row who had taken seven years! Of course, I thought, "Well, I'm afraid I'm going to be the one to spoil your record." But just like the TM Fairfield group, most of these people had had years and years of living in spiritual communities, many with Saniel's teacher, Adi Da. In my eyes, they had paid their dues in the spiritual world and had earned the awakening.

I took up once again with the thought of striving, thinking, "I must try harder." More meditation and more spiritual reading followed which was necessary and provided the discernment I needed to move into a greater understanding of the process. I felt I needed to pay my spiritual dues. The cosmic joke is that letting go and surrender are key in reaching the goal. In a recent Jyotish astrology session, the reader noted the existential angst around my spiritual striving I had put myself through for years. She pointed out it will all come naturally. Effort does not enter in. She said, "I see it reached a peak in 2011." I said that was the time of an awakening and a shift in my awareness and greater understanding of consciousness. She nodded.

That week in November 2004, I had many moments of "what the hell am I doing here?" Followed by "oh, okay, maybe this is possible for me." But once again my "not good enough" feelings arose when I overheard Saniel talking with a woman about her Christian beliefs carrying her into awakening. I was too timid and unsure to share my Christian story with him. But my stolen moment of their conversation planted a seed in me and a hope that my Christian life would come into play sometime.

The most valuable and healing insight of my life happened at our final day small group meeting. I see myself sitting in the comfortable brown leather chair in front of the fireplace of the main meeting hall. It was here that I saw the essence of my relationship with dad. What's the question? How could you transform one of your most painful relationships? I didn't consider my relationship with my dad painful, but I had wished for a closer more attentive relationship. But as I sat there and actually gave it serious thought, I was struck with the recognition that dad had been a solid steady unchanging background in my life. Where I had been feeling a lack because of a yearning for more attention from him, there came instead this recognition of his solid support, sort of my own microcosmic Shiva to mother's Shakti.

It was overlooking Tamales Bay that Carl had the beginning of his second birth. As he stood with his eyes closed, the sense of his body receded into the background and he had a moment when he realized he was awareness, like an eye looking at him and he was the eye/I. The thought shot through his mind with a thrilling sensation of knowing that there is no separation in consciousness. It was an 'I AM THAT' realization. Later an image of being confined in a medieval prison cell appeared. Then as in a panoramic movie shot, he saw the whole castle grounds and realized that the door was open. All he needed to do was walk out.

I didn't feel it yet, but the fire of Saniel's White-Hot Yoga of the Heart had been lit in my Being. I was beginning to cook, physically, mentally, and spiritually. The alchemical process of turning myself into authentic gold had begun. Was Saniel the wizard who set the process in motion?

But first there were more worldly challenges we needed to face.

Carl and I both started to feel a further discontent in our daily lives. What was simmering? That's when the possibility of the pub arose. In hindsight, I see starting this business was born of a need for a final full on karmic exchange and burn off. Once again my character would be tested. There were more lessons to learn, more debts to be paid. Carl had become exhausted with his job of family counseling, mostly within the Department of Children and Family Services. So when my brother had an option to buy a property next to his winery business with the vision of turning it into a pub, we broached the subject of being partners. But I'll never know how I was able to withstand the intense experience of owning this business.

# CHAPTER 13

# The Pub

*H*ere I was in another kitchen, standing over another old Viking stove, but this time it was one I bought myself. Though it was a gorgeous October Sunday, I could feel in my gut that this would be a day of "being in the weeds" to quote Anthony Bourdain. This day I knew I couldn't carry on much longer.

Four years before, in the spring of 2005, Carl and I, along with my brother, Bill, and his wife, Gloria, opened The Piasa Pub in the river town of Grafton, Illinois on the scenic Great River Road. The pub was the ground floor and basement of an old two-story house a few hundred yards from the convergence of the Illinois and Mississippi rivers. We spent nine months remodeling the one hundred year old house, including hiring a contractor to handcraft a polished oak bar. We had found the perfect shade of burgundy to paint the antique pressed tin ceiling and the walls were a warm tan. Our first purchase was the used Viking stove with eight burners and a flat-top grill. The local Mennonite furniture store had the perfect solid oak tables, benches, and short pub stools. We later changed the first deck on the side into a sun room and added an upper and lower deck with colorful umbrella tables and flower boxes along with a second bar. In back was the concrete patio and bandstand. We provided a stage for many talented local musicians, each with their own following. Our pub became a popular venue year round. The first warm days in April, to the colorful leaf peeping days of October were our busiest months. On cool fall afternoons, patrons enjoyed the warmth of the stone fireplace in the downstairs room. Then in January and February, the eagle watchers arrived to view the bald eagles that rode the ice chunks down the river. Our sunroom was usually filled then with people enjoying hot chocolate and spiced hot cider, eager to spot the wintering eagles.

The kitchen was where I spent most of my time. I rarely ventured out. True to my pattern of not wanting to be seen, I didn't need to hear the praise from customers and I certainly didn't want to hear their complaints. I wasn't cooking to feed my ego. Creatively, I put myself into the food. We didn't dump any prefab frozen food into a deep-fat fryer. Occasionally, we would lose a customer because we didn't have French fries. But we made up for them with returning customers who loved our Italian beef and pulled pork barbecue. I made most of the salad dressings from scratch and used fresh herbs in the Thai slaw and basil salad. My artichoke dip and salsa cheesecake were popular appetizers. The first year I tallied close to 2,500 appetizers served in July alone. After that, I didn't count them.

Although owning a bar and restaurant had never been a dream of Carl's or mine, we threw ourselves into it. I was not afraid of food. I had run my own catering business 15 years before with two friends and had had plenty of experience preparing large quantities of food for the church dinners.

Hindsight has shown me that this endeavor was a subconscious choice "to do more," those infamous words from long ago. It was my nagging inner voice speaking to me once again, urging me onward in my search for I knew not what. Like the alchemists of old, how could I change "metal into gold" without getting in the fire? This challenge proved to be another part of my "digging to find my authentic self."

This day Sylvia, a pudgy, not so attractive girl, just out of high school, stood working the flat-top. Over time she had become sullen and passive-aggressive in her slowness to throw more burgers and chicken on the grill as I called out the orders. I had discovered early on if I was not in the kitchen to facilitate the orders, the cooks would only look at one ticket at a time. They didn't want to be rushed. If your life is an endless string of orders on the wall, maybe you see no reason to rush. There'll always be one more order. But this was my establishment and I wanted satisfied customers who didn't have to wait too long.

I understood this was a dead-end job. We could not pay our employees enough to make them loyal and steadfast workers. I could see the end of Sylvia's time with us on the horizon. They all moved on. They would become as worn out with us, as we became with them.

The same was true of Jeannie. When she first started working for us, she had been grateful for the job and she was very good in the kitchen. Her sandwiches looked luscious, piled high with ingredients. Her baskets were consistently neat and generous. But Carl had made the mistake of having her be a server one day. She got a taste of the money she could earn in tips. That taste of tips turned her into poor kitchen help. I had seen it happen before with other kitchen staff. So this day she was a server.

Through our many conversations shared during long hours of chopping salad, stirring sauce, or waiting for the beef to cook, Jeannie confided that she and Sylvia were lovers and had moved in together, along with Jeannie's two autistic sons. I had also learned about her heartbreaking life. She told me about the indifference of her father and the nonexistent relationship with the father of her boys. It was not hard to figure out she had issues with men. Thus she had issues with Carl.

It was early afternoon and we were getting slammed. The bar was full. The handsome, cocky young bartender was a chick magnet. The girls in their camisoles and tank tops lined the bar, sipping the slushy fruity drinks he whipped up. Every table in the sunroom was taken. We were turning tables one after another. Most tables on the upper and lower decks and patio were filled with people basking in the sunshine, listening to George, a local favorite, play his guitar. His soulful tunes were an excellent draw on Sunday afternoon.

A tense atmosphere was ramping up, I could feel it in my body. It was a feeling beyond the usual anxiety of being overwhelmed with keeping up with orders and praying that the supply of food would last the day. On Jeannie's several passes into the kitchen, I could tell she was taking on an attitude. She was complaining about customers and the fact that her section of tables on the patio was the farthest from the kitchen.

Then it happened. I heard her shout at Carl, in front of all the customers "Where's the ice? There's not enough ice! You are so stupid! You don't know how to run a business!" Without leaving my station where I prepared baskets with salad, chips, and condiments, I shouted, "Get out and never come back!" Although I was facing a wall with five rows of tickets with orders to be filled and served, I could no longer ignore her bad attitude and disrespect.

Carl looked stunned at my taking charge of the matter, but he was in agreement. She had been hateful to him since her arrival that morning. With a shocked glare, she turned on her heel and pushed her way past the bar.

Then when I thought the situation could not get worse, it did. Sylvia collapsed in front of the stove. Earlier in the year, she had had a seizure and fallen between the kitchen door and the bar. Luckily, there had been a nurse at the bar who immediately jumped off her stool and took over. On that day, Jeannie had knelt beside her, begging her not to die. By the time the ambulance had arrived, Sylvia had regained consciousness.

This time, however, I knew it wasn't a seizure. It looked like a panic attack. She was hyperventilating and red-faced from the extreme heat of the kitchen. Still not leaving my spot, I told the next person who came through the door (I don't remember who), "Go get Jeannie. She's headed to her car. She's going to have to come back and take care of her."

When Jeannie rushed back into the kitchen, she said hysterically, "She's having a seizure. It's your fault!"

"No, she's not having a seizure. She's just upset about you. Take her into the cooler, get her cooled off and calmed down. Then both of you leave."

Meanwhile, I was confronted with a pub full of hungry customers and a wall full of tickets. There was nothing I could do but continue. I had to ignore the knot of panic in my own gut and the exhaustion in my limbs. Then a pretty young girl hopped off her stool and said," I can help you." Gratefully, I accepted her offer. I instructed the servers to stop taking orders and tell new customers the kitchen was closed due to an emergency. I knew it would take every last bit of energy I had left to work through the forty tickets on the wall.

A couple of hours later, I sat staring off down the river, watching the slow-moving barges, too exhausted to speak. We had been here four years and this had been my worst day. For months Carl and I had become increasingly exhausted trying to keep up with all aspects of the business. Three new bar businesses had opened near us, making competition for customers harder. On Memorial Day weekend, the beginning of our busiest time, the State Police set up a roadblock at the Grafton visitor's center and continued excessive patrols along the River Road all summer. The competition for customers increased further as word got out. "Don't go to Grafton." Breaking even was a challenge that required more of our time and energy, so that we could lower expenses. We were frustrated dealing with the turnover in employees and the inability to find good replacements. This episode with Jeannie and Sylvia was the final straw.

Our hearts were calling us elsewhere. Carl and I had decided that we were going to move to be near our daughter, Kate, her husband, Keith, and our first grandchild, Brady, at some future date. Now seemed like the time. Shortly after that horrendous Sunday, I had a heart-to-heart conversation with my brother about finding a way for us to leave the pub. Bill owned a winery business next door to the pub that his son managed. After we left, he combined the two businesses under one roof. The place is still thriving today.

There had been more than one opportunity for us four owners to fall out. We had survived the closing of the pub for more than a month in the midst of the busy summer season due to a major flood that left three feet of nasty river water in the basement. When disagreements over time, money, and sheer physical exhaustion could have caused a rift in our family, we did not let it happen. We emerged with our family affection intact. We had remained generous with our employees throughout, always letting them have meals and paying more than minimum wage. Now it was time to move on.

# CHAPTER 14

# New Beginnings

May 19, 2010, the moving van was loaded, both cars were jam packed. I made one last pass through the house, grabbed up Mini Me, our fat calico cat, and we were on our way. I did not shed one tear. I had made my peace with leaving long before this day. I knew it was time to let go of this place, this attachment. I followed the example of my dad. He knew when to let go. He had left farming and the farm in a natural progression of his aging. He was not a man of denial. I watched him tear down two barns. These were two majestic buildings that had passed their usefulness, barns that he had spent his life in, milking cows, storing grain, stacking hay, tending his stock. He moved into each new phase of his life with resolve and grace. I would, too.

Elburn, the westernmost suburb of Chicago, was the perfect spot for Carl and me, three miles down the road from Katie, Keith, and Brady. Though Annelise was not due to arrive for another three weeks, she was born the next day after our move. What a welcome!

To the west of us lie familiar scenes of productive farmsteads with lovely homes, fields of corn, soybeans, and wheat and pastures of horses. Five miles to the east is Randall Road, lined with any store you can name. Downtown Chicago is a train ride away 42 miles east. What had we done to earn this good fortune, to have a mature life well lived. Looking back I see the stage was set for my next spiritual level of development.

For so many years we had felt we were in a spiritual wasteland. Toward the end of our Pub days I had given up attending church and playing the organ. I had run out of energy to do both on Sunday. We had a comfortable condo overlooking the Mississippi River and the lure of resting there on Saturday night after a long hard day in the kitchen was too strong. In reflection, I see it as a gentle way of breaking my attachment to my home church. Our first Sunday in Elburn was our first Sunday at the Unity of Fox Valley Church. My first exposure to

Unity was in 2000 when Kate and Keith lived in Mt. Prospect. Kate started attending Unity Northwest in Des Plaines and we looked forward to going to church with them on our visits. Unity teachings provided the combination I was waiting for, Christian teachings and mysticism in a form I recognized.

Scriptures had greater meaning for me when viewed through the lens of Unity. "Behold, the kingdom of God is within you." I began to understand this as insights came to me in meditation. Nothing will come from "out there." No one needs to intercede. God is not "up there" in heaven waiting to work some magic on a repentant sinner. Spirit is here as a constant guiding force manifesting through me to bring invisible good into expression. Grace flows continuously if you open yourself to it. Unity author and pastor, Eric Butterworth, wrote in *A Quest for Truth*, "God is you." Do not look outside or away for anything to happen or to bring to bear on you from without.

Within a month of being in Elburn, spirit led us to receive our first hug from Amma, the "Hugging Saint" from Kerala, India. I had first heard of Mata Amritanandamayi, translated as Mother of Immortal Bliss, from my Waking Down mentor, Karen Steen. Amma brings unconditional love into the world one hug at a time. As we drove to the Westin Hotel in Lombard that day in June 2010, I was curious and open to the experience. How could one woman give millions of hugs to people all over the world? It is a phenomenon that must be observed. As I saw the hundreds of people in the hotel ballroom I wondered, "How is it possible?" Yet when I was in her arms it seemed as if I was the only person she would hug that day. There was no rush as she held me close and murmured in my ear. The attendants helped me to my feet and guided me to a seat nearby. As I sat gazing at her, I felt an unexplained longing to stay close to her. I knew something beyond words had happened as tears came to my eyes and my body vibrated. I knew I had made contact with a God-realized Being.

# CHAPTER 15

## There is no inside or outside, there just is...

" $\mathcal{I}$ hope I can get something out of this besides being barraged with warnings to watch out for the devil around every corner or listening to too many sin and salvation talks," I thought as I pulled into the five hundred car parking lot of the suburban Baptist mega-church. It might be a pleasant experience and a chance to meet new people at best, or tedious at worst. It was certainly a place I would have to be careful how I expressed my beliefs. Little did I know that here would be the trigger for the elusive second birth spiritual awakening that I had longed for since meeting Saniel.

It was a bright September morning and we had been getting settled in Elburn over the summer. I had been attending Unity church since the first Sunday of our arrival where I had found my "tribe" and understood well its positive, mystical, Christian principles. But when an old friend from home invited me to attend her church's women's Bible study, I accepted her kind invitation. I knew we would have fun visiting afterwards, at lunch. My friend greeted me at the door of the huge new church and we joined one hundred women of all ages in the downstairs meeting room. We sat down at a table in the back and settled in for the first part of the morning to watch a DVD presentation by Beth Moore. On the cover of the Bible study guide "Beloved Disciple, The Life and Ministry of John" it says of Beth: "Her joy and excitement in Christ are contagious; her deep love for the Savior, obvious; her style of speaking, electric."

I was hooked from the first sentence of her dynamic delivery. It was not the content of the message, far from it. It was just what the description of Beth said that moved me. She modeled for me a joy, deep love, and enthusiasm for Christ that I had not allowed in my body. It wasn't that I lacked the longing for Christ, but that I had not carried it all the way deep into my heart with a personal passion. The passion that Mary had for Jesus that put her at His feet. This is something of the same passion that Saniel had been describing in his teachings on the "White-Hot Yoga of the Heart," I had just been unable to feel what he meant. I was plagued with my old voice, "I don't get it." It all seemed so elusive.

One day shortly after starting the Bible study, I had an insight during meditation about how aloof and abstract my seeking and practice had been. I thought of Beth Moore's passion and real human emotion in her relationship with Christ. I saw that this passion was what I needed to bring to my practice. I was suddenly moved by a deep and true longing, an impassioned yearning. I begged, "Please show me! Feel me! Be me! I Am – love me – me – love Me – I am the bride – dazzle me – feel, feel, feel – yes! I feel it, a yearning to be filled with spirit! I am that feeling!"

BINGO! ZEAL! I had been missing Zeal. Zeal is one of the twelve powers in Unity teachings. Enthusiasm is the word for zeal used in Siddha Yoga, to be possessed by God or Divine inspiration. Yogananda said in his book *How You Can Speak to God*, "To coax Him to give Himself takes steady, unceasing zeal. When your heart-call is intense, then He will come." These words set off my early memory of singing "Into My Heart" which I hadn't thought of in years.

I see now, this was the beginning of the embodiment of the Divine that I had asked for as a child in the words of this song. "Come into My heart, Lord Jesus." In Psalms it says, "When I pray, You listen. You hear me!" Words I started to believe with zeal.

Deep meditations followed almost daily. Insights flowed. On this day after meditation I wrote, "You are not separate. Do you feel it? Feel it! You are His. You have His Divine spark in you. Feel it. JOY! No boundaries, you are it. Feel the joy! This is where you have longed to be. I am love. My language is music, my soul calls and longs for the angel voices." Yogananda describes faith as the limitless power of God within you. He says, "God knows through His consciousness that He created everything; so faith means knowledge and conviction that we are made in the image of God." For me, this means unbounded consciousness, oneness.

After all these years I began to have the feeling that I was bringing someone to meditation that wanted it, and Being was thanking me for ignoring the babble. At times I felt as if someone else was breathing me. I recognized how blessed I was to have a gentle peaceful path and I began to trust in Being. Each day energy filled my body and I understood the scripture of the vine, the branch, and the fruit as one energy flowing through all. Be God, knowing Himself.

All my insights about no boundaries, flowing energy, faith and trust in Being, were approaching the confirmation of the second birth realization. I began to make progress when I said to myself, "I don't care if anyone agrees with me. This is my truth." The key was to own it. I began to have sensational energy dreams, feeling my body soaring. The dreams included light with glowing yellow, gold, white, and silver misty clouds with sparkler fireworks, accompanied by overwhelming feelings of expansion into consciousness.

Then it happened, my moment of grace, October 21, 2010, 3:00 a.m. I awoke to these words. "There is no inside or outside, there just is…" THERE IT IS! I thought of Saniel's teachings on Onlyness and felt his transmission. I became an observer of this statement and its accompanying feeling. Surprisingly, I fell back asleep and then woke again a short time later with the same words, "There is no inside or outside. There just is."

Following this came the insights into Saniel's teachings on the sacred marriage of awareness and energy, and the nonduality of our existence. I knew I had always been this awareness, and I was infinite and finite simultaneously, what Saniel terms the core wound and simultaneous wellness. Immediately, the meaning of terms that had eluded me began to make sense, like greenlighting and the landing platform. Terms that mean different things to each individual. The greenlighting meant I could confirm for myself that I could own my understanding of this phenomenon of being Divine and human. My landing platform, the belief system that made sense to me, could indeed be my years of faith in a Christian tradition. My home in Christ, my years of service in my church, my Bible, brought me to this moment. My incorporation of my Christian beliefs and Eastern mysticism was a valid landing platform. As I lay there in bed, I felt the front of my body being opened into love and peace.

At last, my second birth. A birth, just what the word implies, a beginning, the coming into awareness of the self-realization of the Divine within me. The creation of a new life requires a man and a woman, so the same is true of the birth of a Divine child. The masculine Shiva, transcendent awareness, requires the union with the feminine Shakti, embodiment energy, to complete the creation. God requires a Goddess.

This is not just a transcendent experience held in awareness, as taught in many Eastern traditions, but an embodiment of the Divine, into the feminine, manifested as matter, Mother. The creation of the Divine made possible by uniting the awareness and energy, feminine and masculine, Shakti and Shiva, embodiment and awareness coming together in creation of the Divine child. We are all Divine, let's always pray to remember.

A few weeks into the Bible study we discussed Psalms 63:5-8 and I was struck by its similarity to my second birth experience. "… I think of you on my bed, and meditate on you in the watches of the night; for you have been my help, and in the shadow of your wings I sing for joy."

I had the insight one day in meditation that part of me was sitting there with great joy as a quiet background. Thoughts would pass through. One by one, these passing thoughts occupied my mind. It became much easier to let the stream of thoughts go without reacting. Thought was going on in a bigger space, a more peaceful space. But in between the thoughts who then notices? What doesn't change? I began to strongly sense the witness, the knower, the part that does not change. I began to honor the noticing and the knowing. This knowing is the recognition of consciousness. Jack Kornfield wrote, "If you can rest in the knowing, the pure consciousness, there's not much more to do." This consciousness is awareness we're using every day. It is so sheer that it's unnoticeable, because it IS THAT which is noticing.

Over time, this concept of consciousness has settled into my body and I think of it as a great mystery. Joseph Campbell wrote, "Life is like arriving late for a movie, having to figure out what was going on without bothering everybody with a lot of questions, then being unexpectedly called away before you find out how it ends." Each lifetime is but a blip on a screen. We are not our story. We have had hundreds of stories. We are mysterious spiritual beings on a journey of an inevitable evolutionary return to our infinite state. I view it as an eternal process. The significance of each of these lifetimes is to move into the authenticity of each lifetime to bring about the knowledge of oneness for all beings. Simply put, the reason for our existence is to manifest LOVE in the world. Along the way, my purpose has come to me. To just be. Hold this sacred space that when I am present with love, it radiates into ALL.

"I've been born during this time to help usher in the golden new age! The Age of Aquarius! La la la, smooth sailing!" When I returned to my spiritual path in earnest, this is what I naively thought. But as we move further into world terrorism, climate change issues, and political chaos, I see more clearly the dire need for holding the sacred space. We were born to this age to carry the message of oneness, to hang on.

Krishnamurti wrote, "Self-knowledge has no end – you don't come to an achievement, you don't come to a conclusion. It is an endless River."

# CHAPTER 16

# Thank you, Spirit

hy had it taken me so long? I was stuck until I became mindful of what was real and true for me. What was real and true for me was bigger than the Christian doctrine I had held. Yet my path was not merely about turning East either. Even through the first years of Waking Down I was trying to fit into the wrong mold, one of totally Eastern thought, though I didn't yet see that Waking Down didn't fit that mold either. I was trying to put 'new wine into old wine skins'. What I needed to do was integrate the two. I prayed and practiced my rituals, but the essence of the message kept eluding me. Joseph Campbell wrote, "The myth we are respectfully worshipping on Sunday will not be the one that's really working in our heart. But once we are willing to embody the sacred in our lives, our maturing can proceed. We can say in effect, I already know I'm a child of God. The question is, how can I be an adult of God?" When I realized I had been numb to joy and lacking in zeal, I decided to let go of old thoughts of lack and stopped saying "I don't get it", and then grace began to flow for me.

Why had I stayed in the church? I had held out hope that awakening could occur there. What I didn't realize at the time was that one half of the equation was being left out and, in fact, denigrated in some churches. The Divine Mother, the manifestation and embodiment of the Divine on earth, is not mentioned in the patriarchal religions. I had been ignoring my discomfort around the subject. Privately, I remember thinking or actually knowing that celebrating so few 'women of the Bible' was missing the mark. But I did not feel wise enough or spiritual enough to speak up and risk showing my ignorance. The feminine had been left out of hyper-masculine religious structures for eons, despite the fact that Jesus himself allowed Mary to remain at His feet.

Indeed, how could centuries of theologians ignore the significance of Mary, possibly Mary Magdalene or Lazarus and Martha's sister, Mary, being the first person He appeared to after His resurrection? It is true that images of the Virgin Mary are present in every Catholic Church, and that her position is highly venerated. Though she is honored and beloved, she is never mistaken for God. In fact, many Protestant religions scoff at the Catholic veneration of Mother Mary. And we know Eve was blamed in the Garden of Eden story from the beginning.

But in the metaphysical sense, Adam and Eve both stepped away from the tree of knowledge into duality. The tree of knowledge represents the oneness we were in the beginning with the Word. Yet creation is impossible without the mother. Equally important as God is the Goddess. She brings forth the manifest world in which Spirit is able to be embodied into a total Divine creation on earth. There is a need to remember, "In the beginning was the word, and the word was with God; and the word was God," but "the word was made flesh and dwelt among us." No mother – no baby!

As I sat reveling in my gentle internal vibration, I reflected upon how mothers lovingly rock their babies with an unconscious gentle motion. Whether they are sitting or standing with their babies does not matter. If their babies are sleeping, fussing, or cooing, rocking comes naturally and comforts both mother and baby. Rocking is an instinctual signal of love. Through the years I had had many flashes of joyful recognition of knowing I was being held. The vibration that had been with me so long was like a whisper, "I am here."

Kundalini is the power of the Goddess. The Divine feminine unfolds perfectly for each individual. Kundalini is not an "it" or a force from someplace else, it is always operating as the power that keeps us alive. Kundalini can be activated in many ways, prayer, meditation, or physical practices. The external manifestation of this life force or Shakti is the Divine helping us recognize and experience the oneness, and remember our Divinity.

I had never studied Kundalini until the day that her power put me on the floor. I guess I had not given her the proper due. She needed to get my attention. On this day, May 2, 2013, I had a full body Kundalini experience. I was not blown disturbingly open, but only given a gentle reminder of the Divine Mother within me. For some people, this experience can resemble psychosis, but I felt guided and protected somehow. As I sat in meditation with the Unity music, I opened to the sensation of the strings, which represented the masculine awareness to me, and the flute which represented the energy of love or feminine, calling each other to my heart. "Come into the heart of this one."

Four days prior to this I had done a shamanic healing with Jeffrey Backstrom, a Waking Down teacher. We had practiced a breathing technique called Breath of Fire that had been very difficult, which I hadn't been able to do, but suddenly "something" spontaneously took over my rapid breathing. She was breathing me. My legs started to jump, my head began to shake, sounds were coming out of me, and my hands started to move in unfamiliar mudras, or poses. My body began to feel like a wind tunnel as the breathing went on and on. As the music ended, a voice said "Get on the floor!" At this point, I felt an orgasmic energy in my lower chakra, followed by a breathing into the navel chakra. Then I realized the energy was moving up my body. There was rapid breathing at each chakra, so I focused my awareness on each chakra, in my heart, in my throat, then the third eye, and finally at the crown when I began wailing and crying. All the while, I asked my guides to stay with me and I was not afraid. Intuitively, I asked to bring them back to my heart. The words, "the body knows," a concept in Waking Down that always baffled me, suddenly made sense. Later I learned that bringing the energy back to the heart is important in grounding the experience.

For YEARS I had been longing for a tangible experience. Thank you, Spirit!

Jeffrey told me three things to move forward with. First was trust. Trust that the experience was true and significant. Second was to keep the awareness with the body. Third was to realize that this was the Divine working with me, in me, as me, and to let her create the program. He also cautioned that the next thing could be anywhere from more cool stuff, to feeling awful as I might release old "junk," to flatness as all gets gradually integrated. But trust that it's all moving me forward. Now three years later, I can say I have experienced each of the things he cautioned me about. Mostly I experience my gentle daily vibration as a reminder of the Divine Being that I AM.

# CHAPTER 17

# "Many Paths, One Heart"

*I*'m so nervous, with sweaty palms, and butterflies in my stomach. I must be having a flashback to my own recital days. The studio is filled with excited and fidgety students and anticipating parents and grandparents. Brady and Annelise will soon perform in their first piano recital. Each little girl is dressed in her best Christmas finery. "Grandma, can I wear your Santa pin?" Annelise asked. So I took it off my sweater and put it on her red velvet dress. She must not be as nervous as I am or she covers it well. Brady looks sharp in his newest Christmas sweater and a Santa hat. He is very quiet, uncharacteristic for him.

As the youngest student, Annelise was first on the program. She marched to the front without hesitation and played "Jingle Bells" perfectly as a duet with her teacher. Brady was equally confident and outwardly calm as he placed his music on the piano. Yes! "Deck the Halls." Great job, what a relief; no mistakes. A proud Grandma moment, but beyond that, I am grateful they have an interest in music and some ability. Music has played a major role in my life and spiritual growth. My hope is that it will in theirs, also.

For me music was the way of leading me to my authentic self, my Mary self, the expression of the Divine. The music evoked spiritual emotion within me, but it then took the discriminative awareness to turn the process into fuller understanding. This means to me that music speaks directly to the spiritual heart by drawing us into Divine awareness. I can see how my first memory being the desire to sing "Into My Heart", was a foreshadowing of the power music would have in my life. Music brings me out of numbness, enabling me to feel the sheer joy of sound. Repressed feelings surface, allowing me to move beyond the mundane. My experience of the power of music preceded my understanding, but through discernment and by inquiry, I see how music moved me beyond mere feeling into a direct experience of the Divine.

"Music is moral law. It gives soul to the universe, wings to the mind, flight to the imagination, and charm and gaiety to life and to everything." – Plato

I first heard of Tim Wheater in Julia Cameron's book on creativity called "*Vein of Gold.*" Her advice was to find a piece of music that brings to your heart an absolute sense of safety. For her it was Michael Hoppe's, *The Yearning*, which featured Tim Wheater's incomparable flute. I immediately ordered the CD. It changed my life. I discovered I could sit in meditation easily as I listened. I can trace back my first awareness of my gentle Kundalini vibration to the early 2000's when I started listening to this music. Cameron says "*The Yearning*" cracked open her heart the first time she heard it. I know what she felt. Gradually over the years I moved away from listening to music in meditation because I thought I was "cheating." It made it too easy. Now I am able to move into the silence and experience the same awareness and sensation with or without music.

Then in 2010 I rekindled an interest in Tim Wheater after rereading *Vein of Gold*. I discovered he had been part of Annie Lennox and the Eurythmics for a while. He had suffered a strange chemical paralysis and could not play his flute. That was when he healed himself with his voice. I wanted a new CD of his work and Spirit led me to *In Unity*. I was drawn to the title after we had been attending Unity church since our move to Elburn that year.

From the first notes, my meditation took on a different dimension, an instant awareness of Spirit filled my body and expanded my consciousness. The awakening themed album was instrumental in what Saniel terms the second birth recognition. Though I have listened to the CD hundreds of times in meditation, it never fails to expand my awareness and set up the gentle vibration within my body. Tears arise at the same point each time as the strings and flute fill my soul in the Peace section of the CD.

This day in February 2016, turned out to be a deepening of what Saniel calls the second life. As I was meditating, I felt this beautiful music fill my space, not just in my ears or head, but within the lightness and hollowness of my body. I had never made an inquiry into this euphoria. I had been sitting here for fourteen years experiencing this phenomenon! Spirit said to me this day that it was time for some integration! What is it? What am I feeling? What does it mean? Images and sensations started to flow: the wind in the willow tree in my side yard, the white puffy June day clouds flowing across an indescribable blue sky, the memory of holding my daughter for the first time, the first sip of cocoa with marshmallows AND whipped cream, the delighted smiles of my grandkids as I bring out the ice cream treats, the purr of my fat calico cat, the loving embrace of my husband, the comfort and safety of my home. All of these sensations and images were evoked by the music. Don Campbell, another sound healer, described this awareness as "an acute sensing in an awakened powerful internal space."

After answering my inquiry about what I was sensing, Spirit said look at *Vein of Gold* again. I turned directly to this quote from Rudolf Steiner, "When the human being hears music he has a sense of well-being, because these tones harmonize with what he has experienced in the world of his spiritual home." There it is!!! The confirmation of music's significance that I had been searching for, but knew already in my heart.

I was reminded of a passage I had read many years before from Dr. Michael Newton's book, *Destiny of Souls*, based on research into spiritual hypnotherapy, as clients recalled their experiences between lives. "From my research, I have come to believe that more than any other medium, music uplifts the soul...it is the language of the soul..." In this case study he asked the client about her experience of Oneness. She described hearing a sound, a reverberating deep bell sound, like an echo. Dr. Newton pressed her, "An echo of what?" She replied, "A mother... full of love...singing to her child."

The body knows what the mind sprints around or struggles with believing. I have a feeling of well-being as I listen that goes beyond my body, yet also includes it. There is joy that blooms in my heart and spreads throughout my chest into my throat, pulling a smile onto my lips, rising upon my cheeks with tears springing in my eyes, opening the top of my head and flowing out with light and bliss. I don't often examine the details of this experience. Healing takes place within sacred space and hints of realizations arise. Today Amma's words came to me, "The creator and the creation are one." Another way of saying it, "God is you." This is different than saying "You are God." It feels different.

One day as I sat cozily in front of my altar, these words floated through my mind. "This is where it starts. This is where it ends. Be the Divine presence you already are." I could hear my heart beating. I went into my heart space and knew my heart as the "Heart", the one "Heart." It felt as big as the universe. As I continued to feel into this joy, I had a recognition of, "Yes, of course, this is IT." My daily vibration continued and I was reminded that I am held in Love. More tears of love and joy came from my being. I felt as hollow as a reed. The heart beat fuels everyone and everything. This is our link to oneness if we only knew it. I realized that the heartbeat I was sensing was a Divine feeling beyond the persona.

I began to feel through my "not enough" limited-ness anxiety, into an essence of myself as powerful and worthy, as worthy as Mary. This instant felt as euphoric as my second birth experience.

About a month after this experience of heart

opening, Saniel and Linda were in our home for a weekend retreat. Saturday morning they shared the beautiful Snatam Kaur song "Heart of the Universe." The few words are simple, but a powerful statement of the truth of our existence.

"There is a space that exists with us, that surrounds us, where angels sing on rays of light, and loves pours forth from the Heart of the Universe." It was no coincidence that those very words had been spoken to me already. I was transported back to the moment of Heart realization I had experienced a month earlier.

Ram Dass said, "The spiritual journey is individual, highly personal. It cannot be organized or regulated. It isn't true that everyone should follow one path. Listen to your own truth." This was mine.

I discovered the secret to following my own path to my truth in a message from Namkai Norbu, a Tibetan Buddhist Dzogchen teacher. Carl had studied his teachings for many years. I found Buddhist teachings complicated and dry, and the practices difficult, but I cannot deny their power. One night I had a dream in which Norbu came down the aisle of my childhood church. When he looked at me, fire shot out of his hands as he held them out to me. I began to move into the light. Like what so often happened with my energetic light dreams, I awoke from being overwhelmed by the power.

My second Norbu dream followed a Waking Down weekend before my second birth confirmation. In the dream, I was lined up with several participants on a retreat. Norbu walked along the line and looked at each of us. As he approached me, I stared intensely into his eyes. "Do you see me?" I asked mentally. "Yes," he acknowledged as he moved on. He then returned and asked a question about a practice. I told him Carl probably had one I could look at. "No, here." Then he tore off a small sheet from a pad containing printed prayers. "You have your own."

I have learned to take note of dreams as an example of imagination since studying Unity's twelve powers, one of which is imagination. Jesus used the power of visions to inspire converts, most notably Saul. Unity founder Charles Fillmore stated that "the simple and universally intelligible avenue of visions and dreams, the work of the imagination, was adopted as an important means by which believers were called together and instructed." Tibetan Buddhism also relies on the guidance of the inner voice, dreams or visions.

When Carl learned that Norbu was coming to his Tsegyalgar East Center in Conway, Massachusetts, he said he wanted to attend. I said I would go, too, not to attend the retreat, but to take the opportunity to see Cape Cod beforehand. I was not registered for the retreat, but when Carl told the organizer about my Norbu dreams, he welcomed me to the opening night address.

The auditorium of the center was crowded, close, and too warm with little air conditioning. Despite my discomfort, as Norbu entered the hall, I felt a sudden opening in my heart and vibration in my body. I strained to make out what he said through his heavy accent, but then he caught my attention when he mentioned other teachers, Jesus, Krishna, and Buddha.

His simple statement about unifying your teachers answered the question I had been struggling with for some time, especially since experiencing Amma, working in Waking Down with Saniel, and renewing my Christian faith at Unity church. Was I being disloyal to any one teacher? Was I confusing myself with more teachings, books, and teachers? Each teaching has led me along my path. Each provided a key understanding to unlock my process. Now in hindsight, the answer is obvious, but then I was still sorting out and developing my discerning wisdom. The energy, the message, the journey, the destination, can be unified. All is one. I feel I have left no stone unturned to arrive at my truth of the nature of the way.

# CHAPTER 18

# At Amma's Feet

*s I watched the fresh marinara sauce bubble up in the huge pot, I was once again standing at an old Viking stove. This time it was in mindfulness and seva service in devotion to Amma. On this Saturday at the end of summer 2016, I was making pizza sauce in the ashram kitchen for 130 participants of Amma's AYUDH conference weekend. Young people had arrived at the ashram from Seattle to Washington DC, to unite in this conference of Amma's international youth group. The theme this year was "One World, One Home." Our hope is in the convictions of the young people of the world to advance peace and prosperity on a global scale.

The ladies in their colorful saris chattered in Hindi around me. I smiled back at them. Then they realized I didn't understand a word they'd said. "Oh, we were just talking about..." Their kindness to me and obvious devotion to Amma radiates to all and I don't feel left out even when I don't understand what they are saying. As I stirred the sauce I felt a loving awareness bubble up in my heart and spread out across the kitchen. I felt love for each of the people cheerfully working, preparing the food for that day, as if their joy was my joy in oneness. My transforming Martha's ways into Mary's devotion in that moment overcame me with tears, as I stood there.

Two years after my first hug with her, Amma established an ashram four miles from our house. Carl and I saw it as a signpost. We immediately became part of the community. Though nothing about the Hindu customs, prayers, chants, songs, or rituals feels familiar to me, my faith in the knowledge of who I believe Amma to be compels me to be part of the community. When a Being of this magnitude came to my backyard I knew I must be there. The only explanation I have is that my Being recognized Amma's Grace as another step in my journey into my heart. Her Embracing the World organization generates millions of dollars for humanitarian efforts throughout the world. One hug at a time, unconditional love flows and I wanted to be part of that. As I have performed my seva I have realized the need for the integration of Martha and Mary. Of course, people need to be fed both physically and spiritually, but devotion to the task and the reason for the task must come from the heart first. It is a matter of attitude. With this realization, I felt all the years of my work in the church transform into a lifetime of devotion. I was devoted to my church which represented my love for Jesus tucked away in my heart. It was loving devoted service all along. The service hadn't transformed. I had.

In 2014, Carl and I agreed to be co-chairpersons of the staff room seva during Amma's tour. This seva involves stocking and serving food around the clock for the three hundred sevites that travel with Amma. Some of the sevites prepare the thousands of meals needed to feed the people who come for their hugs. Others man the booths of items offered for sale, the proceeds of which go to finance schools, disaster relief, soup kitchens, orphanages, and hospitals throughout the world. These people work long hours and appreciate our efforts to provide food and drinks.

Being in charge of the staff room is a seva no one wants to do, mainly because it is long hours with endless clean up and prep, all in a building away from the hall where Amma presides. This year, in advance of the tour, we prepared two thousand cookies, six hundred muffins, six hundred brownies, tubs of hummus, gallons of yogurt, and twenty pounds of granola. In addition to serving and prep, there is purchasing food for three hundred people for three days. I am grateful beyond words for Preet and Raman Johar who labored equally alongside us, as without their help we could not have persevered. I understand that everyone wants to be close to Amma when she is present here. But I also understand that I am close to her always in Spirit, if not physically. Our Pub experience seems to have been a foreshadowing of this responsibility. We are not afraid of large amounts of food. Was I being the ultimate Martha here? I don't think so, because the service is coming from my heart. I have transformed Martha's ways into devotion.

In devotion and service there is surrender. As I approached Amma for my hug this year, I surrendered all to her and mentally acknowledged her great sacrifice in bringing her unconditional love to earth in the form of her dharma. When great Beings come to earth they still have physical bodies with limitations, and sacrifice human needs and comfort. She hugged Carl first and put sandalwood paste on his third eye. Then she hugged us together after putting sandalwood paste between my brows. She spoke to me in Malayalam for the longest time, as she gently rocked us together. I knew in my heart that she was thanking us for our seva and blessing it. I felt like a little child as I cried in her arms.

How does an ordinary Midwestern Christian woman arrive at the feet of this incarnation of Divine Spirit? Through our surrender to staff room seva, we were rewarded by grace in performing the paada puja ritual at Amma's feet. As Carl anointed her feet, I held the hem of her sari. My grandson, Brady, helped me select a gorgeous silk fuchsia cloth trimmed in gold, sold at one of the tour booths, for Amma to stand on.

A beautiful woman named Lakshmi helped us prepare for the ceremony. First we selected a sari to put down under the cloth I had purchased. We found a perfect match in the colors of a sari Amma had worn, from a collection made available just for this ceremony. As part of the ritual, Carl placed two fuchsia roses at Amma's feet.

Lakshmi had lovingly picked them out to match the pants of my first Indian outfit called a shalwar kameez. Earlier that afternoon, I had felt like I was dressing for the prom, as I put on the gold kurta trimmed in fuschia and then draped the matching dupatta over my shoulders. My ashram friends said I looked beautiful and teased me,

"She's not going to want to stand at the stove now!" Lakshmi explained that my part was the envy of all. She encouraged me to surrender to Amma and receive the grace of being at Her feet. She also added that the instructions say not to touch Amma's feet but with a twinkle in her eyes she said, in those two minutes I shouldn't let this rare opportunity pass me by. So as I swept the hem of Amma's immaculate white sari aside, I gently brushed Her feet, as I breathed a prayer of surrender to Her.

In John 12:2-8 is the story of Mary anointing Jesus's feet as Martha served. Once again, Jesus defended Mary, this time for putting the precious oil on his feet instead of selling it for the poor. Indeed, in Mark 14:9 he said, "Truly I tell you, wherever the good news is proclaimed in the world, what she has done will be told in remembrance of her."

My journey to Mary (which I equate with putting on Christ Mind) is one of remembering who I truly am as Divine. Through this ordinary lifetime there has been breakdown, breakthrough, integration, and now glimpses of transformation. Within this ordinary life I am also Divine. When I had come to my moment of grace on that night of my second birth experience, I had to let go of the ordinary to realize the extraordinary. There is no boundary or separateness. There is no outside, no inside, just total consciousness always and ever present. It was when I let go of numbness and dullness and allowed in the zeal of joy, that my moment of grace occurred. Hadn't I felt the gentle vibration of God's love in my body for a decade? I was now ready to accept it as "the gift from God" (John 4:10) that it was.

This quote on truth by Emilie Cady, New Thought author and contemporary of Emerson, Emmett Fox, and the Unity founders, Myrtle and Charles Fillmore, expresses best the goal of miraculous transformation. "Truth – the same Christ lives within us that lived in Jesus. It is the part of Himself which God put within us, which ever lives there with an inexpressible love and desire to spring to the circumference of our Being, or to our consciousness as our sufficiency in all things. The Christ in you, *is you* at the point of God." Our Unity pastor, Rev. Jan Little, often quotes Colossians 1:26-27 , "…the mystery that has been hidden throughout the ages and generations but has now been revealed to his saints…Christ in you , the hope of glory."

Jesus said, "The one who believes in me will also do the works that I do and, in fact will do greater works than these." (John 14:12) In Genesis 1:26-27 it states we were created in God's image and likeness.

Recently I told a lady about our experiences with Amma and extolled her greatness when she said, "You know, you are the same as Amma. She just has a bigger gig!" It's time to use that truth and the confidence that comes from that truth. Now stretches ahead of me the task of continuing on the journey.

# CHAPTER 19

## The Lower Lights

Since the early years of being in Waking Down, I have listened to many interviews on Buddha at the Gas Pump on YouTube. BATGAP is the work of Irene and Rick Archer from Fairfield, Iowa. They have interviewed scores of spiritual teachers and leaders. Coincidentally, Irene and Rick are Amma devotees and Irene took part in the paada puja I described earlier. I didn't know Irene before that night, but as we sat visiting before Lakshmi gave us our instructions, we discovered our connection with mutual friends in Fairfield, Waking Down and now Amma. She told me she selects the interviewees for BATGAP and Rick interviews them. She told me she often selects them intuitively. One such pick was Sat

Shree, an American God-realized teacher. His interview on BATGAP had triggered my thinking on the next stage of my journey. He said, "Get in the boat to continue the journey on this eternal evolutionary path. Don't mistake an island for the farthest shore of your destination." This advice rang out as truth to me from the first time I had heard it. It struck a deep place in me, a knowing place that has always told me awakening is an eternal process.

Sat Shree likened it to crossing a vast ocean. We don't know where we are on this ocean. We may have just left the shore or perhaps we are nearing our destined home. My quest is to discover my place and pace on this voyage. Each period of my life moved me forward. Each "island" a necessary glimpse into the innumerable lessons to be learned in order to imprint the GPS needed to guide my soul into the light. I just need to stay the course until I know that I am God knowing himself. Charles Fillmore, Unity's founder, says in *The Twelve Powers*, "…a great creative plan is being worked out in which the Deity is incarnating itself in its creation."

The maps of this voyage are available to all. Unity says the Bible is the metaphysical revelation of our evolutionary process back to Oneness through spiritual awakening. Sat Shree has noted that the Bhagavad Gita is also the revelation of our journey back to Source. He calls Sri Aurobindo's, *The Mother Book,* the handbook for accomplishing the journey. The keys of becoming Mary are defined in the book and show how to collaborate with the descending energy and consciousness of Spirit, in order to prepare the body to become a channel for this God force. It starts with an unfailing aspiration. It has always been part of our souls' evolution to show that we can be human and Divine together, not one or the other.

Sparked by this aspiration, Aurobindo says there are four key principles. We need to move into a total and sincere surrender. We must stay with our self-opening to the force. We must make a constant and integral choice of knowing the truth of this force. We must choose a constant and integral rejection of falsehoods. The human part of us cannot move past ego driven obscurities, the "I wants" of what is only good for me, my money, my house, my family, my country. We need look no further than five minutes of tv news or one click on a Yahoo feed to see the evidence of rampant egotistical views.

*The Mother Book* says the Divine part of us has to do the work beyond the ego. The human part can't do it. Our human job is to turn toward the Divine and grasp any Divine part that comes to us as impetus to stay on the path. Make a prayer to remember the journey and turn toward grace. Then move forward in your own authority.

Perhaps one of the most difficult concepts to grasp is renunciation. Renunciation is one of the twelve Unity powers. "I release false or limited beliefs and all that is a distraction to my spiritual unfoldment." In other words, the habitual attachments to physical and emotional comforts make us afraid to continue the journey. Some of the most confusing passages in the Bible center around this message. Jesus said in Matthew 10:34-37, "Do not think that I have come to bring peace to the earth; I have not come to bring peace, but a sword. For I have come to set a man against his father and a daughter against her mother, and a daughter-in-law against her mother-in-law; and one's foes will be members of one's own household. Whoever loves father or mother more than me is not worthy of me; and whoever loves son or daughter more than me is not worthy of me; and whoever does not take up the cross and follow me is not worthy of me. Those who find their life will lose it, and those who lose their life for my sake will find it."

Besides renunciation of peace and family, there are verses about giving up attachment to wealth. Matthew 6:19-21 says, "Do not store up for yourselves treasures on earth...For where your treasure is, there your heart will be also." Matthew 19:24 continues, "Again I tell you, it is easier for a camel to go through the eye of a needle than for someone who is rich to enter the kingdom of heaven."

Leonard Cohen sang of the struggle of the journey in my favorite song "Suzanne." The verse about Jesus as a sailor reaching out to "drowning men" creates a yearning within me for Jesus's truth to be understood.

Jesus knew the drowning men were the seekers, the men and women longing to awaken from the "sea of the illusion" of the ego-driven masses around them and the sense of separateness which creates the delusion. So he made all men "sailors" and gave everyone instructions for the voyage. But long before conscious awareness was a possibility for all, the weight of his wisdom was too heavy to bear for most. The truth of his message "sank like a stone." However, a stone does not evaporate, it is still there to be recovered.

The recovery of Jesus's message is brilliantly reflected by Cohen in the chorus of this verse as a deep and abiding longing when you realize you've been touched by the Christ Mind.

The Unity power of Divine Order has been revealed to me over and over in messages, experiences, and teachers I needed all along the way as they appeared in Divine Order for me. I feel blessed to recognize this fact. One such message came one day while browsing the

Internet. The profound poem of awakening by Kahlil Gibran, "The Coming of the Ship," illustrates the nature of the continuing journey. Almustafa had been in the city of Orphalese for twelve years and had looked to sea every day in hopes of seeing his ship that would take him back to the isle of his birth.

The longing for the return trip has been the seed of desire in me as the seeker throughout my life, whether a conscious knowledge or not. The desire for self-realization springs from Source as the impetus to continue. In Almustafa's awakening and returning home, his soul is full of joy, yet there is sorrow in letting go of attachments. The same is true for us, the ego finds the leaving almost unbearable. As the people lament his leaving, Almustafa questions the ways he can impart to them his wisdom about the journey he is ready to embark upon. "Am I a harp that the hand of the mighty may touch me, or a flute that his breath may pass through me?" The harp and the flute have been powerful tangible aids for me. I experienced "his breath" passing through me in my Kundalini experience. He continues, "A seeker of silences am I, and what treasure have I found in silences that I may dispense with confidence?"

It is in the silence of meditation that Spirit has guided me to the deepest insights that have moved me forward in my journey. Emilie Cady spoke of this truth, "When you have learned how to abandon yourself to Spirit, and have seasons of doing this daily, you will be surprised at the marvelous change that will be wrought in you without any conscious effort of your own." Finally when the people ask Almustafa to share his truth, his reply is also "our hope in glory." "People of Orphalese, of what can I speak of that which is even now moving your souls?" Almustafa is speaking of the longing of every soul, whether conscious or unconscious, to make the journey into awakening to our truth.

So in my quest to continue my journey, our journey, Carl and I went to Sat Shree's Fire & Heart retreat. Was this a boat I should board? For six days we meditated three hours a day. There were daily morning and evening talks on "The Path of Love." Over the week Sat Shree's elaboration on the steps on the path of love resonated emotionally and physically in me. He emphasized that our capacity to experience Divine love is directly related to our ability to love as a human being. I understood his message that it is through our trials, troubles, disappointments that we learn the lessons necessary to travel the spiritual path. I saw where my letting go of major attachments and facing disappointments and hurts created the "qualities of human maturity; humility, acceptance, patience, and forgiveness." "I heard an echo of longing to develop in me a mature human heart.

Sat Shree described the mature human heart in this way, "The mature heart surrenders to what IS. It gives selflessly without question. It endures calmly and patiently because it is in connection to the inner peace that comes from within, from the maturity, the natural wisdom of a life lived well." I thought about how often I had dealt with these issues in my years in Waking Down. How I had been tempered in my reactions and guided through my most difficult times in letting go of attachments.

Galatians 5:22-23 also reminds us of the attributes of a mature heart. "The fruit of the Spirit is love, joy, peace, patience, kindness, generosity, faithfulness, gentleness, and self-control. There is no law against these things."

In the last hour, on the last day of the retreat, I had the transcendent energetic experience I had hoped for. The night before Sat Shree had drawn a diagram of a circle full of squiggly lines that represented the content of our lives, at times chaotic, but always full of activity, emotions, and reactions. The emptiness beyond the circle was the background, our knowing background, the ground of our Being. The lines represented the "who we are" of our story. The rest is the "what we are." The diagram was similar to one of Saniel's representing what he labels the core and periphery.

Toward the end of the talk Sat Shree said, "Seeing existence just as it is, without content, is awakening." At that moment the comment triggered a knowing recognition of existence. The euphoric feeling continued as I stepped outside, I felt my body and awareness expand into the surroundings of nature and vast sky with a sensation of no boundaries. I began to feel the impersonal fact of being part of this beautiful existence. The sky, the trees, the birds, and I were one. As I felt into it further, I added in my own mind, "minus my story." This deepening of the experience of I AM THAT is what Saniel calls "personification of the awakening cosmos. In that stage of the journey, one goes beyond mainly identifying with the unawakened persona and even awakened personhood, to come forth with one's divinity and carry it into the world." A nineteenth century Unity leader, Imelda Shanklin, in her book, *What Are You?*, said until we can answer this question correctly without reference to personal data and defining ourselves in a personal manner, we cannot be truly happy because we do not know completely what we are.

I stopped taking for granted the miraculous power of the universe and truly opened my eyes to all creation. Things that I had given little thought to suddenly began to astound me. From the birth of a baby to the daily sunrise, all became new, mysterious miracles. This is existence.

On Saturday afternoons throughout junior high and high school, my job was to find a hymn for the opening of Sunday school every week. As Sunday school super-intendent, mother led the opening and I played the piano. As I sat in meditation one day, the words to one of mother's favorite old hymns, "Let the Lower Lights Be Burning," came to mind. I saw my reluctant teenage self, plunking out the song on the old, out of tune upright piano in the church fellowship hall. I sense now how the messages of these cherished hymns sunk into my heart. After this memory I went on a search of the bookshelves to find the old Sunday school songbook. The hymn had long ago been removed from the newer hymnals. Philip P. Bliss, a famous 19th century composer, wrote this hymn shortly after a ship crashed on the shores of Lake Erie when the pilot missed Cleveland harbor. The upper lighthouse beacon was dimly shining through the storm, but the lower shore lights that marked the opposite side of the harbor opening were not shining at all.

> Brightly beams our Father's mercy
> From His lighthouse evermore;
> But to us He gives the keeping
> Of the lights along the shore.

Let the lower lights be burning!
Send a gleam across the wave!
Some poor fainting, struggling seaman
You may rescue, you may save.

When I started to play the hymn on my keyboard, my vision blurred with tears as I realized how blessed I have been. I am the struggling seaman and the lower lights. I said a prayer of gratitude to mother for her part in my journey.

Soon after moving to Elburn I had a vision-like dream of holding sacred space. I saw a matrix surrounding the world with each awakening being occupying a part of the grid. We filled that space with love. I heard the words "release yourself to be that love in the world." My purpose, our purpose, as human beings is to continue bringing forth happiness, love, and compassion. We must hold our sacred space in this matrix of love until it spreads and we reach the tipping point. Then we will each rescue, we will save.

# CHAPTER 20

# Love Divine

*T*he final edits for *Into My Heart* were completed some time ago and it was sent to be published. A problem with the ISBN kept arising. Each time it was a different problem. Instead of becoming frustrated or impatient I rather felt, "This is interesting. There must be a reason for the delay. All will happen in divine order." It turns out what I thought was the end of the book was not the end. I continue to believe this is an eternal process and a wondrous mystery.

Right now the Divine is calling – nay, screaming for us to hold sacred space. As we sink into further deepening political, global, and environmental chaos, the need for manifesting the Divine becomes greater and greater.

Incivility has become the order of the day on social media, TV, news, and on the street. I have, for the first time, personally witnessed people feeling emboldened to be rude to people unlike themselves. Greed has taken an even firmer grip on society. The lack of compassion for others, and the lack of common sense to solve the problems we face, leaves my heart aching. The call came from within me to see how I might be of service to the Divine in the world today. I knew it must start with me first. How could I actually manifest the Divine in myself?

As I stated earlier in the book, my second birth awakening has continued over the years. My meditations began to expand my conscious awareness. Now a felt sense of a tangible vibrational force arises when I turn my attention inward. I knew silence was the key to coming into contact with my higher self, my inner self, my soul, my Being, call it by any name. Healing is returning to a state of alignment with your higher self or true way of being. To become still and silent outwardly and inwardly is the key. Sat Shree says the power in silence is primal. In silence, we will be in contact with the quality of what we are and not who we are. It is where we can set aside "me." Finding this quality is the purpose of life and the spiritual path.

Unity co-founder Charles Fillmore emphasized in *Teach Us to Pray*, "the necessity to withdraw into this deep stillness of the soul." Fillmore's wife, Myrtle, called this the secret place of Spirit. She says in her book, *How to Let God Help You*, "We are turning from the world of the outer and are coming into the wonderful place which is called 'the secret place of the Most High.' Psalms 91:1."

Jesus said in Matthew 6:6 "When thou prayest, enter into thine inner chamber, and having shut the door, pray to thy Father who is in secret." In the silence is where I have felt Divine presence. There, the perfect, unchanging part of you, your Being, is where you connect with God. Ultimately it will be discovered that the Life Force we call God is what we are. We are not separate from the Divine. It is not enough to know this with our mind. In this silent place I experienced Spirit, I felt oneness, I sensed God's guidance. For me, it has taken on a magical quality. When a question arises in meditation, an insight will come, and sometimes even an answer from a book or recording.

Carl and I were drawn to attend our second silent retreat with Sat Shree and his wife, Satyamayi, at Lake Tahoe. The center for the retreat was located near Squaw Valley in the beautiful Sierra Nevada nestled among the towering pines. Canyons of eight-foot snow banks lined the paths of the retreat center, and the roofs of the buildings were topped with foot upon foot of snow after a season of record snowfall. The power of the setting added to the power of presence. Each participant carried the flow of their process, each unique, but mutual in intent.

The days started at six a.m. with one-and-a-half hours of meditation, followed by two more meditations at eleven and four. Sat Shree calls these times silent sittings. We do not repeat mantras or try to maintain difficult postures. We just sit within his powerful transmission of Divine force where transformation is possible. Between the sittings, silence is maintained as much as possible. After lunch, we met in small groups to share our experiences and questions. Two hours in the evening was spent with Sat Shree as he shared the points of the path of unconditional love established in us as a path of devotion to the Divine. Devotion feeds the longing for God. As pointed out in *The Mother Book*, aspiration is the first step on the spiritual path. Surrender is the final stage of letting go of the ego's control.

On the first day of the retreat, my small group met with Sat Shree. Here we each had the opportunity to ask our personal questions. Even though I had not previously emailed or Skyped with him about my questions, I had discovered that if I listened, answers came, either during meditation or on one of Sat Shree's recordings. He had told us the focus of his teaching would be the Bhagavad Gita and Sri Aurobindo's, *The Mother Book*. Listening to his commentary of these books became magical to me. Questions were always answered. When I told him this he said, "Yes, actually, you and Carl are both quite linked with me."

Then I described my inner vibration which had been activated and developed in my years with Saniel and Linda Ma. I indicated that through the years it had risen from the base of my spine to chest level, the heart. From my earliest years of spirituality in Radha Swami, I had been waiting for light and sound in a transcendent experience through the third eye and crown chakras. I have learned this is not the entire goal.

In referring to the vibration Sat Shree said, "That's perfect. Stay with your heart. Your devotion is already there. Now attend to connect with God. Be infatuated with God. It is as intimate as making love. It engages the whole body and that's the fire. Devotion brings the Self to faithfully focus on the Divine. It will carry on. Feel the movement because your system is opening to the Universal. Then God starts coming and will accelerate the process. Devotion is a prayer, and God cannot help but come to you. When it is felt like it is in you, it is very powerful. Take that to your meditation. Be a groupie for God!" As he told me this, I remembered the teaching in *The Mother Book* about collaborating with the descending Divine to become manifest in the body. God is you, but you must let him in. Blow on the Divine spark to ignite the fire. Sat Shree points out that having the humility and faith to accept where we are on this path is necessary and all part of surrender. He says, "The seed gets planted when you meet a realized being and when he recognizes receptivity in you."

In Eric Butterworth's book, *Unity: A Quest for Truth*, he wrote in the chapter titled 'Emphasis on You', "We are innately spiritual beings and have an insatiable hunger for Truth through which our hearts are ever restless until they find repose in the knowledge of God. But regardless of where or what the religious expressions might have been all through the ages, the confidence that there is a power or powers to help has lit the fires on every altar, built every temple, made every creed articulate and supported every prayer."

Later that evening, Sat Shree shared his teaching "The Path of Love" as the path of devotion. "It is a means of focusing our emotional nature on the Divine. In the process, we become Divine's lover and the Divine becomes our beloved." Similarly, Saniel taught that this "dropping into the heart" is foundational to the experience of awakening to the Divine.

The next morning in meditation the magnificent hymn, *Love Divine, All Loves Excelling*, by Charles Wesley, founder of Methodism, came to me. When I returned to my room I looked up the words and listened to the Mormon Tabernacle Choir sing it. Wesley had, to my mind, experienced and understood the nature of transformation. As I listened I had a shift in consciousness and broke down in sobs with the realization that all my time in the church had been in devotion. All the music, organ playing, and singing were transformed into devotion and a knowing of God's love for me and my love for God through these words, "Pray and praise thee without ceasing, Glory in thy perfect love… Lost in wonder, love, and praise." I clearly saw and sensed how much the Divine loved me all that time, and that my devotion to the church had been my love for the Divine. Just like my years of cooking were transformed at the ashram stove, as my awareness spread out over the kitchen, this moment encapsulated those beloved hymns into love for the Divine.

I held this knowledge in my heart all week, thinking how much it meant to me. But the Divine Mother had one more momentous experience for me where I went to the root of my devotion. I awoke at 4:15 a.m. on the last day of the retreat with the beautiful words of the hymn, *Love Divine*, still resonating through me. Suddenly, another Kundalini experience began. For more than an hour, Shakti energy ran through my body, rapid breathing started, and tears erupted. As I held on to Carl, wave after wave moved through me. I realized it wasn't just my Martha time in the church that had been lived in devotion, but my whole life, from my gentle birth and being born into the stability of seven generations of grounded ancestors, to the present moment. My life as a daughter, sister, wife, mother, and grandmother, every hymn I had ever played, every child I had ever taught, every meal I had ever prepared was transformed into devotion. The knowing of my true nature gave me the knowledge that my "story" had carried me here. I remembered Sat Shree's words to go to the felt sense and experience the movement of what was coming into my body, experience the wonder and build on the sensations being felt. Ignore the mind, it will try to take it away by imposing old habits of understanding.

As the energy continued to pour through my body, I felt an overwhelming love for Saniel and Linda Ma, and the life changing part they had played in bringing me to this stage in my spiritual journey. I would not have come to this moment without the years of their transmission and personal heart-to-heart teaching. I would not have understood the extraordinary quality of this experiential knowing. Sat Shree says this knowing becomes wisdom when you understand it in a 'felt' way.

Kundalini is the Divine Mother's energy of love preparing the "vessel so it can expand and hold the transformation of every part of being, and to let go of the structure of "me." We can know the Divine that has lived every *thing* since the beginning. To expand my "vessel" or body, I participated in another week-long silent retreat at Amma's ashram. It was only the second silent retreat Amma has offered in the United States. She feels that her Western devotees can now benefit from this experience.

Through the various types of meditation, yoga exercises, bhajans (spiritual songs), and prayers, there came a deepening of devotion. Amma has provided emotional support to millions with her hugs and her teachings. While politicians dither, she brings about real change with her worldwide contributions to education, health, jobs, and housing. Amma continuously models for us all, how our spirituality must be an instrument for world peace and truth.

In this lifetime, the Divine has been a constant companion even when I was not aware of it. The Divine was not going to let me go until I realized it for myself. Divine dropped me down in the midst of the most blessed existence of Divine expression with wonderful teachers and teachings both past and present, from Jesus to Saniel and Linda Ma to Unity to Sat Shree to Amma. All are expressions emanating from the same Source.

In the process of writing my story, I have come to see how discernment, practice, devotion, and faith have enabled me to recognize the embodiment of the Divine spark of Presence in myself. The grace of Presence continues to unfold within my "ordinary" life. The purpose of this life – my life, your life – is to expand this Presence so that all beings can know the love of the Divine in Oneness.

I now have clearer answers to my questions about Martha and Mary. Martha was lost in her doing and seeking, just as I had been. She did not understand what Mary did, that by just being in Divine Presence, a felt sense of knowing arises which brings the Presence into your being heart. This is where transformation occurs. Then doing, seeking, being, and knowing become an expression of the Divine which is true devotion.

As I wrote the previous paragraph, my thoughts were lead to this beautiful and poignant old hymn of unconditional love. I am firm in the knowledge that the Divine will never let me go. I am just as firm in the knowledge that as part of the Divine, **I** will never let me go.

"O Love That Wilt Not Let Me Go"

O Love that wilt not let me go,
I rest my weary soul in Thee;
I give Thee back the life I owe,
That in Thine ocean depths its flow
May richer, fuller be.

# ACKNOWLEDGMENTS

I wish to acknowledge the talented editors and designer who helped make this book a reality.

Stephanie Mahron, owner of Angel Editing, www.stephaniemahron.com, was instrumental in the early development of my book. In our first conversation, she directed me to the extraordinary in my "ordinary" story. She clearly and concisely showed me how to "show not tell" in her spot-on editing of my first attempts.

Maureen Barberio, m.a.barberio@gmail.com, brilliantly smoothed transitions in the story, and cleared up any questions the reader might have had about my meaning.

Deborah Perdue, owner of Illumination Graphics, www.illuminationgraphics.com, designed both the cover and interior, which illustrate beautifully the message of transformation in my journey. I extend my deepest appreciation to Deborah for her patience and guidance in bringing this project to life.

www.ingramcontent.com/pod-product-compliance
Lightning Source LLC
LaVergne TN
LVHW051512080426
835509LV00017B/2041